COOL
SHARING

COOL SHARING

Recipes by Louise Pickford

Photographs by Ian Wallace

CASSELL ILLUSTRATED

First published in Great Britain in 2005 by Cassell Illustrated,
a division of Octopus Publishing Group Limited
2-4 Heron Quays, London E14 4JP

A CIP catalogue record for this book is available from the British
Library.

ISBN 1 84403 289 2
EAN 9781844032891

Recipes by Louise Pickford
Photographs by Ian Wallace

Printed in Hong Kong

4

CONTENTS

COOL SHARING

It's never easy after a hard day at the office to come home and cook, especially if you have guests. The temptation to pick up a takeaway or ready meal seems an attractive one, but everyone loves home cooked food. Now your worries are over, Cool Sharing is guaranteed to take the stress out of entertaining so that whatever your budget, culinary experience or time schedule you'll find a huge choice of inspiring dishes to suit any occasion.

Entertaining is fun, it's a time for relaxing, for laughing and sharing anecdotes, for enjoying delicious food in good company. But what to cook? Expand your repertoire so that you can cook something different each time friends come over. With the help of Cool Sharing it's easy. The book is set out into chapters determined by type – Chicken; Pork, Beef and Lamb; Fish and Seafood; Vegetables; Fruit; Eggs and Dairy, making it easy to find the perfect recipe.

Because few of us can afford the luxury of shopping daily for our food, a well stocked 'fridge and store cupboard is essential. This book will show you how sensible shopping will ensure you have a good selection of fresh produce and staples so that even if friends drop by unannounced you can rustle up a delicious gourmet meal with ease.

The great thing about Cool Sharing is that gourmet doesn't have to mean costly. The recipes are designed so that everyday ingredients are combined creatively to produce mouth-watering dishes. There's plenty to choose from with recipes inspired from cuisines around the world. There are simple, quick to prepare dishes for mid-week supper whilst others are more involved for weekend dinner parties when we have more time.

The key to preparing and cooking great meals with ease, is careful planning. Cool Sharing will help guide you through all the basics; what to buy, how best to shop and when. How to store fresh produce safely and how to cook creative, healthy and tasty meals for everyone.

PLANNING

Cool Sharing is a guide on how best to use your fridge, store cupboard and freezer so that there is always something on hand to make a tasty meal, so let's start there.

The freezer

Make the most of your freezer, it can come in really handy for entertaining. Buy fresh stocks and keep them in the freezer; frozen berries are really handy especially when fresh fruits are unavailable or expensive. Pastry cases can be made in advance and frozen. Many completed dishes freeze well and can be made several weeks ahead and thawed the day before.

The store cupboard

Most dishes are made from a combination of fresh and staple ingredients so keeping a well stocked store cupboard means that all you need to buy for your dinner party is the fresh stuff, making shopping a breeze. If guests drop by at short notice, there's no need to panic because with a little creative cooking your store cupboard could even provide you with a meal fit for a king.

When the opportunity arises plan a big shop, one where you buy all those basic items that will ensure you have everything you need. Below is a list of essentials.

Oil - extra virgin olive oil, vegetable oil
Vinegar - white wine, red wine and balsamic
Canned tomatoes - chopped tomatoes are best
Canned fish - tuna in olive oil, canned anchovies
Pulses - chickpeas, kidney beans, borlotti beans
Pasta - spaghetti, penne
Spices, **Salt and pepper** - use sea salt and freshly ground black
   peppercorns and buy a selection of spices
Rice - basmati, Thai Jasmine, long grain and arborio rice
Flour - plain and self-raising are essential
Sugar - caster sugar, soft brown sugar
Asian sauces - soy, oyster, hoisin, Thai fish sauce, sweet chilli sauce
   (refrigerate once opened)
Miscellaneaous - buy capers, olives, mustard (refrigerate once opened)

The fridge

Cool Sharing is a guide to making light of entertaining and your fridge is your new best friend. Shopping for fresh ingredients once a week should ensure that you have plenty of choice for the following 7 days. If you buy a selection of meat and poultry, eggs and dairy, vegetables and fruits you will find it easy to cook up a storm at any time. Seafood keeps for less time than other items and I recommend not keeping it longer than 24 hours before cooking or freezing.

Remember that over-buying is a waste of both time and money. Meat, poultry and fish freezes well, so if you're worried the 'use by' date is approaching, pop it in the freezer. Eggs and dairy last longer, most for more than a week but always check individual packs. Most fruit and vegetables will keep for several days and up to a week in the fridge. See storage tips on how to keep things fresher for longer.

SHOPPING

With good planning it should be possible to shop once a week for most fresh ingredients. If you know when you are expecting guests, shop a couple of days in advance for all your vegetables, fruit, dairy, meat and chicken. Seafood keeps least of all fresh produce and is best bought the day you are cooking it (buy fish ahead of time and freeze, remembering to defrost in plenty of time). Each chapter begins with a sample shopping list so you can see just how easy it is to shop so that you can cook a variety of different dishes.

Supermarkets are super convenient for all your weekly needs. They stock a great range of fresh ingredients from fruit and vegetables to meat, poultry and seafood. If you are lucky to live close to a good quality butcher, fishmonger or green grocer use them. Talk to the shop owner, find out what's best, in season and cheapest. If a recipe requires meat or fish to be prepared in a particular manner your butcher or fishmonger will be happy to oblige.

Shopping seasonally will mean that you are eating fresh produce at its best. Obviously some fruits and vegetables are only availble from overseas, but those grown locally will taste best when they are in season. Not only that, seasonal produce tends to be cheaper.

STORAGE

- Always place uncooked meat or seafood on the bottom shelf so that no raw juices drip down and contaminate other food.

- Place herbs in sealed plastic (zip lock) bags with a splash of water, they should keep fresh for up to 5 days.

- Remove meat, poultry and seafood from plastic wrapping. Place on a plate and wrap loosely with foil.

- Put mushrooms into a paper or cloth bag.

- Store potatoes, apples, onions, bananas and pears in a cool dark place, not the fridge.

- Check 'use by' dates and remember to freeze before that date is reached.

- Freeze meat and poultry for up to 1 month

- Freeze fish for up to 2 weeks

The pictures which open each chapter show meat and poultry uncovered, and the shelves are arranged so that the foodstuffs can be seen clearly. Always arrange your own fridge as described above.

THE RECIPES

All the recipes in Cool Sharing are accessible and easily achievable. Most are quick to prepare and although some may take an hour or more in the oven that leaves the cook plenty of time to relax, take a bath or chat with friends. Many dishes can be made ahead of time, or even the day before so that all that is required on the day is a short time in the oven to heat through. Recipes are colour-coded so that you see at a glance which dishes can be prepared ahead, part-prepared or need last-minute cooking.

Blue is for super simple and is suitable for those who have had little or no kitchen experience.

Red is for quick and easy and requires a basic knowledge of cooking, but nothing too scary or time consuming.

Green is for everyday recipes for those who cook often and are happy to have a go.

Many are designed to be served at the table. There is a wide range of dishes from starters and mains to side-dishes and desserts and many recipes offer suggestions as to what would make the perfect accompaniment.

Vegetarians are well catered for in the Vegetables chapter with a great variety of dishes; some suitable as starters, others make more substantial mains. There are light and healthy salads and tasty accompaniments.

Here is a list of handy tips to make your cooking more enjoyable.

- Find out from guests if there are any special eating requirements.

- Plan ahead so that you have everything you need to hand, any last minute perishables can be collected on the day (at lunch or on the way home).

- Always read a recipe through to the end before you start cooking so there are no hidden surprises.

- Make sure you have all the equipment necessary for each particular dish.

- Prepare in the morning if you have time so that everything is waiting for you when you get home.

- If you are entertaining mid-week have the table laid and alcohol and other drinks chilled before you leave for work in the morning.

Equipment

Because the recipes in Cool Sharing are designed for entertaining it will be important to make sure you have a selection of baking dishes, flan tins and cake tins. These items don't need to be expensive and many larger supermarkets stock a wide range of inexpensive cookware, perfect for those on a budget.

Aside from the basics like saucepan, roasting tin, knives etc. here is a list of more specialised equipment that you'll need for the recipes in Cool Sharing.

- A food processor makes light work of chopping, mincing, liquidizing, pastry making and more, so make the investment, you won't regret it.

- An oven thermometer is essential if you are cooking cakes or pastries.

- A 23 cm/9 in square and 20x30 cm/8x12 in ceramic baking dishes.

- A 23 cm/9in fluted flan tin.

- 4 ramekin dishes.

- An oven-proof casserole. That is one that can be used on both the hob and in the oven

- Electric hand beaters make whisking a breeze.

Now all you need to do is pick up the phone and make a date with friends and impress them with your Cool Sharing meal.

THE STORE CUPBOARD

If you cook every dish in Cool Sharing, your store cupboard will finally include all the items shown in the following pages, in bare necessities and the optional extras and you will be able to conjure up an instant meal at any time. Try to store pasta, noodles rice, flour, sugar, oats and other dried goods in airtight containers. Check 'use by' dates regularly and buy herbs and spices in fairly small quantities as they will lose their flavour over time. Once opened, some sauces, relishes and preserves need to be stored in the fridge. Always check the labels. Don't forget to replace store cupboard staples, like canned tomatoes, anchovies and capers as you use them.

BARE NECESSITIES

Oils
Extra virgin olive oil
Vegetable oil
Sunflower oil

Sauces:
Dark soy sauce
Light soy sauce
Sweet soy sauce

Pasta
Spaghetti
Penne
Tagliatelli

Flour
Self-raising flour
Plain flour

Rice and Noodles
Jasmine rice
Basmati rice
Arborio (risotto) rice
Long-grain rice
Chinese egg thread noodles

Sugar
Caster sugar
Icing sugar
Soft brown sugar
Demerara sugar

Dried Herbs and Spices
Oregano
Sage
Rosemary
Thyme
Parsley
Marjoram
Coriander
Curry powder

Stock cubes
Vegetable
Fish
Chicken
Beef or lamb

Canned fish
Tuna in oil
Anchovies in brine

BARE NECESSITIES

Vinegars
White wine vinegar
Red wine vinegar
Balsamic vinegar

Miscellaneous
Tomato purée
Tomato ketchup
Dijon mustard

Canned chopped tomatoes

Sea salt
Black peppercorns

Bicarbonate of soda
Baking powder

OPTIONAL EXTRAS

Oils
Sesame oil
Hazelnut oil

Vinegars
White vinegar
Rice wine vinegar

Sauces
Hot chilli sauce
Worcestershire sauce
Oyster sauce
Hoisin sauce
Thai fish sauce
Thai red curry paste
Passata sauce
Miso paste
Tahini paste
Laska paste

Chutneys and Preserves
Dark treacle
Honey
Redcurrant jelly
Mango chutney
Blueberry jam
Apricot jam
Clear maple syrup

Dried Herbs and Spices
Ground turmeric
Ground cumin
Ground cinnamon
Ground ginger
Hot chilli powder
Garlic powder
Dried red chilli flakes
Kaffir lime leaves
Chinese five-spice powder

Cayenne pepper
Cumin seeds
Cardamom pods
Star anise
Paprika
Allspice
Cinnamon stick
Whole cloves
Whole nutmeg
Dried bay leaf
Szechuan peppercorns
Shredded coconut
Ground almonds
Vanilla essence
Vanilla pod
Palm sugar

Rice and Noodles
Pudding rice
Flat rice noodles
Vermicelli rice noodles
Dried udon noodles

Canned Goods
Canned chickpeas
Canned red kidney beans
Capers in brine

Extra Extras
Bamboo skewers
Sun-dried tomato paste
Black olives
Green olives
Saffron strands
Preserved lemons
Roasted peanuts
Blanched almonds
Flaked almonds
Roasted cashew nuts
Walnuts
Dried figs

Pistachio nuts
Hazelnuts
Almond essence
Semi-dried tomatoes
Dried porcini
Chinese rice wine or sherry
Coconut milk
Limoncello
Rosewater
Light beer
Dry cider
Guinness
Tofu – plain and smoked
Pine nuts
Sultanas
Frangelico or Amaretto liqueur
Kirsch
Dessert biscuits
Vanilla ice cream
Nutella
Gelatine
Dried breadcrumbs
Cornflour
Couscous
Bulghar wheat
Puy lentils
Orrechiette pasta

CHICKEN

From your weekly shop and your basic store cupboard you can make any one of the chicken dishes shown below. The fresh ingredients that you will need are highlighted in the fridge. Some recipes will need extra ingredients or vegetables to serve which do not need to be stored in the fridge. These are shown on the shopping list. Always read through the recipe you choose to make sure that you have all the ingredients to hand.

RED ONION
GREEN SALAD
MANGETOUT
CHINESE CABBAGE
SWEETCORN
FRENCH BEANS
BEANSPROUTS
SWEET POTATOES
POTATOES
ONION
SHALLOTS
GARLIC
CELERY
FRESH BAY LEAVES
FRESH ROOT GINGER
FRESH ROSEMARY
FRESH TARRAGON
MIXED FRESH HERBS
THAI BASIL LEAVES
KAFFIR LIME LEAVES
SAFFRON STRANDS
LEMONGRASS
CARDAMOM PODS
CINNAMON STICK
DRIED RED CHILLI FLAKES
STAR ANISE
WHOLE CLOVES
DRIED BAY LEAF
NAAN BREAD
DRY WHITE WINE
COCONUT MILK
COUSCOUS
BAMBOO SKEWERS
THAI RED CURRY PASTE
THAI FISH SAUCE
HOT CHILLI SAUCE
LASKA PASTE
FLAT RICE NOODLES
ROASTED PEANUTS
BLANCHED ALMONDS
FILO PASTRY
HONEY
GREEN OLIVES
PRESERVED LEMONS
CAPERS IN BRINE

SPICED CHICKEN SKEWERS
WITH GARLIC SAUCE

Serves: 4
Preparation time: 15 minutes
Cooking time: 12–16 minutes

The skewers need to be soaked in cold water for 30 minutes before they are threaded with the chicken and cooked. This helps to prevent the wood from burning during cooking. The chicken can be marinated for several hours in the fridge. Return to room temperature for 30 minutes before cooking.

1 tbsp ground turmeric
2 tsp garlic powder
2 tsp ground cumin
1 tsp ground cinnamon
salt and pepper
8 skinless chicken thigh fillets (about 175 g/6 oz each)
2 tbsp olive oil
1 unwaxed lemon, cut into wedges
1 red onion, cut into wedges
12 fresh bay leaves

Garlic yogurt sauce:
200 g (7 oz) Greek-style yogurt
1 garlic clove, crushed
1 tbsp lemon juice

4 large bamboo skewers, soaked in cold water for 30 minutes

Mix the spices with 1 teaspoon of salt and a little pepper. Cut the chicken thighs in half and place in a bowl with the oil and the spice mixture and stir well until the chicken is evenly coated. Leave to marinate for 30 minutes.

Thread the chicken pieces on to the soaked skewers, allowing 4 pieces of chicken per skewer, alternating with the lemon, onion and bay leaves. Preheat a ridged grill pan (or conventional grill) until hot, add the skewers and cook for 4-5 minutes each side until the chicken is cooked through. Wrap loosely in foil and rest for 5 minutes.

Make the sauce: combine all the ingredients in a bowl and season to taste. Serve with the chicken.

CRISPY CHICKEN WITH SWEET CHILLI VINEGAR SAUCE

Serves: 4
Preparation time: 10 minutes
Cooking time: 50 minutes

Bird's-eye chillies are the small fiery chillies used in South-East Asian cooking. They are really hot so, if wished, discard the seeds before adding to the sauce.

4 chicken quarters (about 175 g/6 oz each)
1 tbsp vegetable oil
1 tsp salt
1 tsp Chinese five-spice powder
$1/4$ tsp ground Szechuan peppercorns

Sweet chilli vinegar sauce:
2 spring onions, finely chopped
1 bird's-eye red chilli, finely chopped
1 tsp freshly grated root ginger
2 tbsp sweet soy sauce
2 tbsp light soy sauce
2 tbsp balsamic vinegar
2 tbsp water
2 tsp sesame oil

green salad, to serve

Preheat the oven to 220°C/425°F/Gas Mark 7. Place the chicken quarters in a bowl, add the oil, salt, Chinese five-spice and Szechuan pepper and stir well until the chicken is evenly coated. Place the chicken, skin-side up, on a rack set in a roasting pan and roast for 45 minutes until the chicken is cooked through. Heat the grill to high and grill the chicken for 4–5 minutes until the skin is really golden and crisp. Rest for 5 minutes.

Make the sauce: combine the ingredients in a bowl, pour over the chicken and serve hot with a green salad.

CHINESE-STYLE CHICKEN SALAD

Serves: 4 as a starter
Preparation time: 20 minutes

150 g (5 oz) mangetout, trimmed
250 g (8 oz) cooked chicken, shredded
1 carrot, thinly sliced
125 g (4 oz) Chinese cabbage, shredded
2 spring onions, trimmed and thinly sliced
1 large red chilli, deseeded and sliced
1 bunch of fresh coriander, roughly chopped
2 tbsp lime juice
2 tbsp light soy sauce
2 tsp caster sugar

Blanch the mangetout in a saucepan of lightly salted, boiling water for 1 minute, drain, refresh under cold water and pat dry. Place the mangetout in a large bowl and add the chicken, carrot, cabbage, spring onions, chilli and coriander.

Combine the lime juice, soy sauce and sugar in a bowl and stir to dissolve the sugar. Pour over the salad, toss well until evenly coated and serve at once.

ROAST CHICKEN WITH ROSEMARY AND LEMON

Serves: 4
Preparation time: 10 minutes
Cooking time: 50 minutes

If you are concerned about jointing a chicken yourself, either buy the bird from a butcher and ask him to joint it for you, or buy chicken quarters and cut each quarter in half with a sharp knife.

1 kg (2 lb) chicken, jointed into 8
1 onion, cut into wedges
2 celery sticks, chopped
2 garlic cloves, roughly chopped
1 unwaxed lemon, roughly chopped
2 sprigs of fresh rosemary, roughly chopped
salt and pepper
2 tbsp extra virgin olive oil
100 ml (3^1/$_2$ fl oz) dry white wine
1 tbsp chopped fresh celery leaves

Preheat the oven to 220°C/425°F/Gas Mark 7. Put the chicken, onion, celery, garlic, lemon, rosemary, and salt and pepper into a roasting tin to fit in a single layer. Pour over the oil and wine and roast for 45 minutes until the chicken is golden, turning a couple of times with a slotted spoon.

Remove the pan from the oven, transfer the chicken pieces to a warm plate and cover with foil. Carefully spoon off and discard the excess fat from the roasting tin, leaving the pan juices, and simmer gently for 2–3 minutes until reduced and thickened slightly.

Serve the chicken pieces with the pan juices, garnished with the fresh celery leaves.

CHICKEN COOKED IN COCONUT MILK

Serves: 4
Preparation time: 15 minutes
Cooking time: 1½ hours

My mum always used to cook pheasant in a half-milk, half-stock mixture which resulted in the most beautiful sauce imaginable. I thought it would be fun to try it with chicken and coconut milk – it's yummy too. This can be made ahead of time and warmed through on a medium heat for 15–20 minutes until the sauce and chicken are really hot.

1.5 kg (3 lb) chicken
salt and pepper
2 tbsp sunflower oil
400 ml (14 fl oz) can coconut milk
200 ml (7 fl oz) chicken stock
4 Kaffir lime leaves, bashed
1 stalk lemongrass, roughly chopped
4 garlic cloves, smashed
2.5 cm (1 in) piece of root ginger, sliced
2 tbsp soy sauce
1 tbsp soft brown sugar
juice of 1 lime

To serve:
steamed broccoli or mangetout
boiled rice

Preheat the oven to 190°C/375°F/Gas Mark 5. Season the chicken with salt and pepper. Heat the oil in a flameproof casserole and fry the chicken for 10 minutes until browned all over. Remove from the heat and discard all but about 1 tablespoon of the oil. Add the remaining ingredients to the pan, return to the heat and bring to the boil.

Cover the casserole with a lid, transfer to the oven and bake for 1 hour. Remove the lid and bake for a further 15 minutes until the chicken is cooked through and the juices thickened slightly. Season to taste and serve the chicken and pan juices with steamed greens and boiled rice.

CHICKEN KEBABS WITH HERBED COUSCOUS SALAD

Preparation time: 15 minutes, plus marinating
cooking time: 8–10 minutes

Couscous is the main staple of North African countries and is served in a similar way to pasta or rice. It is in fact a pasta-like grain that swells when moistened and is readily available from supermarkets. The chicken can be marinated for several hours in the fridge. Return to room temperature for 30 minutes before cooking.

4 skinless chicken thigh fillets (about 175 g/6 oz each)
1 tbsp extra virgin olive oil
4 tbsp Greek-style yogurt
juice of 1/2 lemon
2 garlic cloves, crushed
1/2 tsp ground cumin
1/4 tsp cayenne pepper
salt and pepper

Herbed couscous:
250 g (8 oz) couscous
300 ml (1/2 pint) cold water
125 ml (4 fl oz) extra virgin olive oil
juice of 1 large lemon
2 tbsp each chopped fresh basil, coriander, mint and parsley

4 bamboo skewers soaked in cold water for 30 minutes

Cut the chicken into chunks and place in a bowl. Add the oil, yogurt, lemon juice, garlic, spices and salt and pepper and stir well to coat the chicken evenly. Marinate for 30 minutes and thread on to the soaked skewers.

Prepare the couscous: place in a bowl, add the water and leave to soak for 10 minutes. Drain the couscous and shake well to remove any excess water. Stir in all the remaining ingredients, season to taste and leave to infuse until required.

Preheat the grill to high and cook the chicken for 4–5 minutes each side until charred and cooked through. Serve with the couscous.

THAI-STYLE CHILLI AND BASIL CHICKEN

Serves: **4**
Preparation time: **10 minutes**
Cooking time: **6–7 minutes**

Thai red curry paste is a ready-made spice mix used to flavour Thai curries and stir-fries. It is available from the Asian section of most supermarkets and all Asian food stores. This dish is best served as part of a meal with other Asian dishes and rice.

250 g (8 oz) French beans
2 tbsp sunflower oil
500 g (1 lb) skinless chicken breast fillet, thinly sliced
1 tbsp Thai red curry paste
4 Kaffir lime leaves, shredded
2 tbsp water
1 tbsp Thai fish sauce
2 tbsp soft brown sugar
a small handful of basil leaves, preferably Thai

plain boiled rice, to serve

Blanch the beans in lightly salted boiling water for 1 minute, drain and refresh under cold water. Pat dry on kitchen paper.

Heat the oil in a wok or large frying pan and, when hot, add the chicken, curry paste, Kaffir lime leaves and water. Stir-fry for 2–3 minutes until the chicken is cooked through. Add the beans, fish sauce, sugar and basil leaves and cook for a further 2–3 minutes until the sauce is thickened. Serve with the rice.

CHICKEN AND NOODLE LAKSA

Serves: 4
Preparation time: 10 minutes
Cooking time: 20 minutes

This is a richly flavoured and hearty soup. Laksa paste is a Malaysian curry paste and is available from the Asian section of most supermarkets or from Asian food stores.

3 tbsp laksa paste
900 ml (1 1/2 pints) chicken stock
1 x 400 ml (14 fl oz) can coconut milk
2 tbsp Thai fish sauce
1 tsp ground turmeric
500 g (1 lb) peeled butternut squash, cubed
500 g (1 lb) skinless chicken breast fillets, cubed
250 g (8 oz) flat rice noodles
4 tbsp chopped fresh coriander
2 tbsp roasted peanuts, finely chopped
125 g (4 oz) beansprouts

To garnish:
2 hard-boiled eggs, shelled and quartered
1 large red chilli, deseeded and sliced

Put the laksa paste into a wok or large saucepan with the chicken stock, coconut milk, fish sauce, turmeric and squash, bring to the boil and simmer gently for 5 minutes. Add the chicken and simmer for a further 10 minutes until both the squash and chicken are cooked.

Cook the noodles according to the packet instructions, drain well and divide between 4 warmed soup bowls. Spoon over the soup, top with the coriander, peanuts and beansprouts and serve garnished with the boiled eggs and chilli.

MOROCCAN-STYLE CHICKEN FILO PIE

Serves: 4–6
Preparation time: 25 minutes
Cooking time: 1 hour

125 g (4 oz) butter
1 onion, chopped
2 garlic cloves, crushed
2 tsp grated root ginger
1 tsp turmeric
1 tsp ground cinnamon
1/4 tsp saffron strands
salt and pepper
600 ml (1 pint) chicken stock
4 eggs, lightly beaten
2 tbsp lemon juice
125 g (4 oz) blanched almonds, toasted
1 tbsp icing sugar
500 g (1 lb) sweet potatoes, peeled and cubed
500 g (1 lb) cooked chicken, shredded
10 large sheets filo pastry

Melt half the butter in a saucepan and fry the onion, garlic, ginger, spices and 1 teaspoon each salt and pepper for 10 minutes until the onion is soft and golden. Add the stock, bring to the boil and cook for 10–15 minutes or until thickened and reduced to about 300 ml/1/2 pint.

Combine the eggs and lemon juice in a bowl and stir into the onion mixture. Heat gently over a low heat, stirring, until the mixture is curdled in appearance. Stir in the almonds and icing sugar and transfer to a large bowl.

Steam the sweet potatoes for 10 minutes until tender, drain well and add to the onion mixture. Add the chicken and stir until evenly combined.

Preheat the oven to 200°C/400°F/Gas Mark 6 and grease a 23 cm/9 in loose-bottom cake tin. Melt the remaining butter in a small pan, brush 1 sheet of pastry with butter and carefully press into the prepared tin. Repeat with 5 more sheets of pastry to line the tin completely, allowing the edges of the pastry to overhang the tin. Spoon in the filling, and fold the overhanging pastry on top. Brush the remaining pastry with butter and crumple on to the pie to form a crust. Bake for 30 minutes until golden.

MALAYSIAN-STYLE ROAST CHICKEN

Serves: 4
Preparation time: 5 minutes
Cooking time: 1^1/$_4$ hours

Pouring boiling water over the chicken to tighten the skin is a method traditionally used when cooking Peking duck (it would then be hung up to dry for 24 hours). This results in the skin becoming really crisp during cooking.

1.5 kg (3 lb) chicken
2 litres (3^1/$_2$ pints) boiling water
2 tbsp honey
3 star anise
1 cinnamon stick, bashed
juice of ^{1}/$_2$ lime
2 slices lime
2 tsp Chinese five-spice powder
1 tsp salt
a pinch of dried red chilli flakes

To garnish:
2 tsp salt
^{1}/$_2$ tsp Chinese five-spice powder
juice of 2 limes

Preheat the oven to 200°C/400°F/Gas Mark 6. Place the chicken on a wire rack set in the sink. Reserve 250 ml/8 fl oz of the boiling water and pour the rest over the chicken to tighten the skin. Thoroughly dry the chicken with kitchen paper and transfer to a roasting tin.

Put the reserved water in a saucepan with the honey, star anise, cinnamon, lime juice and slices, Chinese five-spice, salt and chilli and simmer gently for 10–15 minutes until syrupy and reduced by about two-thirds.

Drizzle the syrup all over the chicken and roast for 1^1/$_4$ hours, basting with the pan juices every 15 minutes until the chicken is cooked and the skin crisp and golden.

Cut the chicken into portions and place on a warmed platter. For the garnish, combine the salt and Chinese five-spice in a small dish and pour the lime juice into a separate bowl. Serve with the chicken to dip.

CREAMY CHICKEN AND MUSHROOM STEW

Serves: 4
Preparation time: 20 minutes
Cooking time: 40 minutes

1.5 kg (3 lb) free-range chicken, jointed into 8 (see page 22)
salt and pepper
25 g (1 oz) butter
2 tbsp extra virgin olive oil
1 onion, finely chopped
2 celery sticks, chopped
250 g (8 oz) brown cap mushrooms, halved if large
150 ml ($^1/_4$ pint) dry white wine
150 ml ($^1/_4$ pint) single cream
2 tbsp chopped fresh tarragon

Season the chicken pieces liberally with salt and pepper. Heat the butter and oil in a large flameproof casserole and as soon as it stops foaming fry the chicken for 5 minutes until golden all over. Remove with a slotted spoon and set aside.

Add the onion and celery to the pan and fry gently for 5 minutes. Add the mushrooms and fry over a medium heat for 3–4 minutes until golden. Return the chicken to the pan.

Pour in the wine, bring to the boil, cover and simmer gently for 30 minutes. Remove the lid, stir in the cream and tarragon and simmer, uncovered, for a further 10 minutes until the chicken is cooked and the sauce is thick and creamy. Serve at once.

ROAST CHICKEN WITH SHALLOTS AND HERBS

Serves: 4–6
Preparation time: **15 minutes**
Cooking time: **$1^1/_2$ –$1^3/_4$ hours**

To ensure the chicken is cooked through, insert a skewer into the thickest part of the thigh, leave for 3 seconds and remove. Test that the skewer is hot to the touch (be careful not to burn yourself) and that any juices that run from the chicken are clear.

> 2 kg (4 lb) chicken
> salt and pepper
> 50 g (2 oz) butter, softened
> 1 lemon
> a handful of fresh herb sprigs, such as rosemary, thyme, sage
>   and tarragon
> 8 large garlic cloves, left whole
> 12 shallots
> 300 ml ($^1/_2$ pint) dry white wine
> 300 ml ($^1/_2$ pint) chicken stock

Preheat the oven to 200°C/400°F/Gas Mark 6. Wash and dry the chicken thoroughly and season inside and out with salt and pepper. Rub the chicken all over with the butter, pushing some up underneath the skin. Halve the lemon and rub all over the chicken and place the used halves into the body cavity, along with most of the herbs and the garlic cloves.

Blanch the shallots in a pan of lightly salted, boiling water for 5 minutes, drain and pat dry.

Place the chicken, breast-side down, in a large roasting pan surrounded by the shallots and remaining herbs. Roast for 15 minutes, turn onto the other breast, baste the bird and roast for a further 15 minutes. Turn the chicken breast side up, baste again and roast for a final 35 minutes or until the chicken is cooked through.

Remove the chicken and the shallots from the pan and wrap loosely in foil. Rest for 15 minutes.

Transfer the pan to a medium heat, add the wine and boil rapidly until reduced by half. Add the stock and boil for a further 10 minutes until thickened slightly. Carve the chicken and serve with the shallots and gravy.

CHICKEN WITH PRESERVED LEMONS AND OLIVES

Serves: 4
Preparation time: 20 minutes
Cooking time: 1$^1/_4$ hours

Preserved lemons are used in North African cooking to add a lovely sharp, sour flavour to stews. They are available from larger supermarkets or specialist food stores. Cook couscous according to the packet instructions as brands vary.

2 kg (4 lb) free-range chicken, jointed into 8 (see page 22)
salt and pepper
2 tbsp extra virgin olive oil
1 large onion, sliced
3 garlic cloves, crushed
1 tsp ground coriander
1 tsp ground turmeric
1 tsp ground ginger
$^1/_2$ tsp ground cinnamon
$^1/_4$ tsp saffron strands
400 ml (14 fl oz) chicken stock
125 g (4 oz) green olives
25 g (1 oz) preserved lemons, chopped
2 tbsp chopped fresh parsley
2 tbsp chopped fresh coriander

couscous, to serve

Season the chicken pieces with salt and pepper. Heat the oil in a flame-proof casserole and fry the chicken pieces for 5 minutes until browned all over. Remove with a slotted spoon and set aside. Add the onion, garlic and spices to the pan and fry gently for 5 minutes. Return the chicken to the pan and pour in the stock. Bring to the boil, cover and simmer gently for 25 minutes.

Stir in the remaining ingredients and cook, partially covered, for a further 15 minutes until all the chicken is tender and the sauce thickened slightly. Serve hot with couscous.

MUSTARD CHICKEN WITH LEMON AND CAPER RICE

Serves: 4
Preparation time: 10 minutes, plus marinating
Cooking time: 20 minutes

If using the grated zest of a lemon it is always best to buy the unwaxed variety. If unavailable, use ordinary lemons but wash the skins well first.

4 skinless chicken breast fillets
2 tbsp extra virgin olive oil
grated zest and juice of 1 unwaxed lemon
2 tbsp Dijon mustard
2 tbsp chopped mixed herbs, such as basil, rosemary and thyme
salt and pepper

Lemon and caper rice:
250 g (8 oz) long-grain rice
25 g (1 oz) butter
1 tbsp capers, drained and washed
2 tbsp chopped fresh parsley

green salad, to serve

Place the chicken in a shallow dish. Combine the oil, lemon zest, mustard, herbs and some salt and pepper. Pour over the chicken, stir well and leave to marinate for 30 minutes.

Prepare the rice: cook the rice according to the packet instructions and drain. Return to the pan and stir in the butter, lemon juice, capers and parsley and season to taste. Cover and leave to infuse until required.

Preheat the grill to high. Remove the chicken from its marinade and grill for 6–7 minutes each side until charred and cooked through. Wrap loosely in foil, leave to rest for 5 minutes and serve with the rice and a green salad.

INDIAN-STYLE BUTTER CHICKEN

Serves: 4
Preparation time: 20 minutes
Cooking time: 45 minutes

This can be made up to 24 hours ahead. Return to room temperature for 1 hour before warming through on a medium heat for 15–20 minutes until the sauce and chicken are really hot.

1 onion, roughly chopped
3 garlic cloves, roughly chopped
2 tsp grated root ginger
150 ml ($^1/_4$ pint) cold water
1 cinnamon stick
seeds from 3 cardamom pods
6 whole cloves
$^1/_4$ tsp dried red chilli flakes
1 dried bay leaf, crumbled
2 tbsp vegetable oil
1 x 400 g (13 oz) can chopped tomatoes
1 tsp salt
750 g (1$^1/_2$ lb) skinless chicken breast fillets, cut into chunks
25 g (1 oz) butter, diced

coriander leaves, to garnish
plain boiled rice and naan bread, to serve

Put the onion, garlic, ginger and 1 tablespoon of the water into a food processor and process to form a smooth paste. Grind the spices and bay leaf in a spice grinder or coffee grinder to a fine powder.

Heat the oil in a flameproof casserole, add the onion paste and spice mix and stir-fry for 5 minutes over a medium heat until lightly browned. Add the tomatoes, remaining water and salt and bring to the boil. Simmer gently, covered, for 30 minutes.

Add the chicken and cook, uncovered, for 10 minutes. Remove the pan from the heat, dot the mixture with the butter and replace the lid. Leave to rest for 5 minutes. Stir well, garnish with the coriander leaves and serve with rice and naan bread.

MUM'S SWEET AND SOUR CHICKEN

Serves: 4
Preparation time: 20 minutes
Cooking time: 1^1/$_2$–2 hours

As the name implies, this is a dish my mum used to cook for the whole family. I love cooking it myself now as both the smell and taste are nostalgic. This can be made ahead of time and warmed through on a medium heat for 15–20 minutes until the sauce and chicken are really hot. You can make this up to 24 hours in advance and refrigerate. Reheat before serving.

> 25 g (1 oz) butter
> 2 tbsp olive oil
> 8 large chicken drumsticks, skinned
> 2 onions, thinly sliced
> 1 large green pepper, deseeded and thinly sliced
> 2 garlic cloves, crushed
> 300 ml (^{1}/$_2$ pint) chicken stock
> 3 tbsp red wine vinegar
> 3 tbsp tomato purée
> 2 tbsp soft brown sugar
> 2 tsp Dijon mustard
> 1 tsp Worcestershire sauce
> 2 tbsp chopped fresh tarragon
> salt and pepper
>
> mashed potato, to serve

Preheat the oven to 160°C/325°F/Gas Mark 3. Heat the butter and oil together in a flameproof casserole and fry the chicken drumsticks for 5 minutes until browned on all sides. Remove with a slotted spoon and set aside.

Add the onion, pepper and garlic to the pan and fry gently for 10 minutes until the vegetables are softened. Return the chicken to the pan.

Combine the remaining ingredients, adding some salt and pepper and add to the pan, then bring to the boil. Cover the casserole with the lid and bake for 1^1/$_2$-2 hours, stirring occasionally, until the chicken is falling from the bone and the sauce is thickened (remove the lid for the final 15 minutes). Season to taste and serve with mashed potato.

MEXICAN-STYLE CHICKEN WITH SWEETCORN SALSA

Serves: 4
Preparation time: 15 minutes, plus marinating
Cooking time: 15 minutes

4 skinless chicken breast fillets
2 garlic cloves, crushed
2 tbsp lime juice
2 tbsp hot chilli sauce
2 tsp ground cumin
$1/2$ tsp caster sugar
salt and pepper

Sweetcorn salsa:
1 head sweetcorn
125 g (4 oz) cherry tomatoes, halved
1 garlic clove, chopped
2 tbsp soured cream
1 tbsp olive oil
1 tbsp lime juice
2 tbsp fresh coriander leaves

extra virgin olive oil, to serve

Lay the chicken breasts flat on a chopping board and, using a sharp knife, cut through the thickest side almost in half but leaving them intact. Open out flat and place in a large dish. Combine the remaining ingredients with some salt and pepper, spread over the chicken, cover and marinate for 30 minutes.

Make the salsa: plunge the sweetcorn into a large pan of lightly salted, boiling water and cook for 10 minutes. Drain well and refresh under cold water. Pat dry.

Cut down each side of the sweetcorn to remove the kernels and place in a bowl. Add the remaining ingredients, stir well and season to taste.

Preheat a ridged grill pan until hot and cook the chicken breasts in batches for 2–3 minutes each side. Rest for 5 minutes and serve topped with the sweetcorn salsa and drizzle over some extra oil.

PORK, BEEF AND LAMB

With a variety of kinds and cuts of meat included in your week's shop and your basic store cupboard you can make any one of the dishes shown below. The fresh ingredients that you will need are highlighted in the fridge. Some recipes need extra ingredients or vegetables to serve which are on the list. Always read through the recipe you choose to make sure that you have all the ingredients to hand.

FENNEL
MANGETOUT
FRESH ROOT GINGER
FRESH BAY LEAVES, BASIL, THYME, MINT, ROSEMARY
PAK CHOY
WHOLE CLOVES
CUMIN SEEDS
BEENSPROUTS
POTATOES
NEW POTATOES
SHALLOTS
ONION
CARROTS
BEETROOT
ORANGE
SESAME BUNS
WHITE BREAD
NAAN BREAD
BULGHAR WHEAT
CHINESE THREAD NOODLES
FLAT RICE NOODLES
PUY LENTILS
COUSCOUS
KAFFIR LIME LEAVES
STAR ANISE
CHINESE FIVE-SPICE POWDER
GROUND TURMERIC
GROUND CUMIN
GROUND CORIANDER
CAYENNE PEPPER
ALLSPICE
PAPRIKA
CINNAMON STICK
OYSTER SAUCE
PASSATA SAUCE
DARK SOY SAUCE
LIGHT SOY SAUCE
THAI FISH SAUCE
THAI RED CURRY PASTE
RED WINE VINEGAR
RICE WINE VINEGAR
TOMATO KETCHUP
TOMATO PUREE
DIJON MUSTARD
CHINESE RICE WINE OR SHERRY
SWEET SHERRY
DARK TREACLE
HONEY
REDCURRANT JELLY
MANGO CHUTNEY
PALM SUGAR
FRESH LASAGNE SHEETS
PENNE
SPAGHETTI
GUINNESS
RED WINE
DRY WHITE WINE
CAPERS IN BRINE
ANCHOVY FILLETS
BLACK OLIVES
ROASTED CASHEW NUTS
COCONUT MILK
FROZEN PUFF PASTRY
SUN-DRIED TOMATO PASTE
BECHAMEL SAUCE

39

ROAST PORK WITH FENNEL

Serves: **4**
Preparation time: **15 minutes**
Cooking time: **1^1/$_2$ hours, plus resting**

1.5 kg (3 lb) boned and rolled pork loin
3 tbsp olive oil
salt and pepper
2 heads of fennel, thickly sliced
150 ml (^{1}/$_4$ pint) dry white wine
2 garlic cloves, crushed
2 fresh bay leaves
1 tsp lemon zest
1 tbsp lemon juice
2 tbsp chopped fresh parsley

Preheat the oven to 200°C/400°F/Gas Mark 6. Rub the pork all over with oil, salt and pepper. Arrange the fennel slices in a flameproof casserole and top with the pork. Add the wine, garlic, bay leaves and lemon zest to the pan.

Roast the pork, uncovered, for 1^1/$_2$ hours, basting occasionally. Carefully remove the pork, wrap loosely in foil and set aside to rest for 20 minutes.

Add the lemon juice and parsley to the pan juices and place over a medium heat. Simmer gently for 10 minutes or until the sauce is thickened slightly. Season to taste.

Carve the pork into thick slices and serve with the fennel and pan juices.

STIR-FRIED PORK AND MUSHROOMS WITH OYSTER SAUCE

Serves: 4
Preparation time: 20 minutes, plus marinating
Cooking time: 7–8 minutes

To cook the noodles follow the instructions on the packet, drain well and place in warmed bowls.

500 g (1 lb) pork tenderloin, thinly sliced
3 tbsp dark soy sauce
3 tbsp Chinese rice wine or dry sherry
4 tbsp sunflower oil
1 garlic clove, crushed
2.5 cm (1 in) piece root ginger, shredded
200 g (7 oz) mangetout, trimmed
350 g (12 oz) shiitake and oyster mushrooms, mixed

Sauce:
75 ml (3 fl oz) chicken stock
2 tbsp oyster sauce
2 tsp cornflour

Chinese egg thread noodles, to serve

Place the pork in a bowl, add the soy sauce and rice wine or sherry and marinate for 15 minutes. Strain and reserve the marinade.

Combine the sauce ingredients in a bowl and stir well until the cornflour is evenly blended.

Heat half the oil in a wok or large frying pan until smoking, add the pork and stir-fry, in batches, for 2–3 minutes until browned. Transfer to a plate and wipe the pan clean.

Add the remaining oil to the pan and, when hot, stir-fry the garlic and ginger for 10 seconds. Add the mangetout and stir-fry for 1 minute, then add the mushrooms and stir-fry for a further 3 minutes. Return the pork to the pan, stir once and then add the sauce and reserved marinade. Cook for 1 minute and serve with noodles.

SLOW-BRAISED PORK BELLY WITH ORANGE AND SOY

Serves: 4
Preparation time: 10 minutes
Cooking time: 2 hours 20 minutes

This can be made up to 24 hours in advance and reheated before serving.

1 kg (2 lb) pork belly strips
300 ml ($\frac{1}{2}$ pint) chicken stock
100 ml ($3\frac{1}{2}$ fl oz) dark soy sauce
50 ml (2 fl oz) sweet sherry
grated zest and juice of 1 orange
2 tsp grated root ginger
2 garlic cloves, crushed
2 bird's-eye red chillies, bashed lightly
2 tbsp soft brown sugar
4 whole star anise
1 cinnamon stick

To serve:
steamed pak choi
plain boiled rice

Put the pork in a flameproof casserole and pour in enough water to cover the meat. Bring to the boil and simmer gently for 20 minutes. Drain and return the pork to the pan.

Add the stock, soy sauce, sherry, orange zest and juice, ginger, garlic, chillies, sugar and spices. Again add just enough water to cover the pork and bring to the boil. Cover and simmer gently for 1$\frac{1}{2}$ hours. Remove the lid and simmer for a further 30 minutes until the pork is tender and the sauce thickened.

Serve the pork and pan juices with steamed pak choi and boiled rice.

BARBECUE PORK RIBS

Serves: 4
Preparation time: 10 minutes
Cooking time: 1 hour

You can use either the racks of pork ribs or the pork belly strips, whichever you prefer. The sauce can be made several days in advance. Keep chilled until required.

1 kg (2 lb) pork spare ribs or pork belly strips
150 ml ($\frac{1}{4}$ pint) white vinegar

Barbecue sauce:
100 ml ($3\frac{1}{2}$ fl oz) passata sauce
4 tbsp honey
2 tbsp dark treacle
2 tbsp tomato ketchup
2 tbsp white vinegar
1$\frac{1}{2}$ tbsp Worcestershire sauce
$\frac{1}{2}$ tbsp Dijon mustard
1 tsp salt
$\frac{1}{2}$ tsp garlic powder
$\frac{1}{4}$ tsp paprika
salt and pepper

green salad, to serve

Preheat the oven to 200°C/400°F/Gas Mark 6. Put the ribs in a saucepan with the vinegar and enough water to cover. Bring to the boil and cook for 20 minutes. Drain well and place the ribs in a roasting tin.

Make the barbecue sauce. Place all the ingredients in a small saucepan, bring to the boil and simmer gently for 10 minutes until reduced and thickened. Pour over the ribs and stir well until evenly coated.

Transfer the roasting tin to the oven and cook for 30 minutes, turning the ribs over half-way through. Cool slightly before serving with a green salad.

STICKY PORK WITH DIPPING SAUCE

Serves: 4
Preparation time: 15 minutes
Cooking time: 30 minutes

Palm sugar, which comes in a block, is a type of sugar used in Thai cooking. It is similar to dark soft brown sugar which can be used instead. Be careful when adding the Thai fish sauce and water to the palm sugar as it will spit.

100 g (3^1/$_2$ oz) palm sugar, finely chopped
50 ml (2 fl oz) Thai fish sauce
50 ml (2 fl oz) water
2 shallots, finely chopped
2 garlic cloves, crushed
^{1}/$_2$ tsp ground allspice
500 g (1 lb) pork tenderloin, thinly sliced

Dipping sauce:
100 ml (3^1/$_2$ fl oz) rice wine vinegar
2 tsp caster sugar
1 large red chilli, thinly sliced

coriander leaves, to garnish

Put the palm sugar in a saucepan and heat gently until melted. Add the fish sauce and water, stirring until the sauce is blended. Bring to the boil and simmer for 5 minutes. Add the shallots, garlic, allspice and pork to the pan, stir once, cover and simmer gently for 15 minutes. Remove the lid and cook for a further 15 minutes, stirring occasionally, until all the liquid is evaporated and the pork is sticky.

Make the dipping sauce: combine the ingredients in a bowl and stir until the sugar is dissolved.

Transfer the pork to a plate and garnish with some coriander leaves. Serve with the chilli dipping sauce.

VIETNAMESE BEEF NOODLE SOUP

Serves: 4
Preparation time: 10 minutes
Cooking time: 25 minutes

1 litre (1³/₄ pint) beef stock
2 thick slices root ginger
1 onion, thinly sliced
2 garlic cloves, sliced
3 whole star anise
2 cinnamon sticks, bashed lightly
2 tbsp sugar
4 tbsp Thai fish sauce
350 g (12 oz) flat rice noodles
350 g (12 oz) beef fillet
vegetable oil

To serve:
2 red chillies, chopped
125 g (4 oz) beansprouts
a handful each of fresh basil, mint and coriander

Put the beef stock into a saucepan with the ginger, onion, garlic, star anise, cinnamon, sugar and fish sauce. Bring to the boil and simmer for 20 minutes and then strain.

Cook the noodles according to the instructions on the packet and drain well. Rub the beef with a little vegetable oil and cook on a preheated ridged grill pan for 3 minutes each side. Rest briefly and cut into slices.

Place the noodles into warmed soup bowls, pour over the beef stock and top with the beef. Serve with chillies, beansprouts and fresh herbs.

COCONUT BEEF WITH CASHEW NUTS

Serves: **4**
Preparation time: **10 minutes**
Cooking time: **8–10 minutes**

Serve this rich coconut beef with other stir-fried dishes such as Sticky Pork with Dipping Sauce (page 45) and Asian Vegetable and Tofu Salad (page 97) as part of an Asian meal.

2 tbsp vegetable oil
1 large onion, sliced
2 garlic cloves, crushed
1 tsp grated root ginger
500 g (1 lb) beef fillet, sliced
1 tsp ground turmeric
50 g (2 oz) roasted cashew nuts
300 ml ($^1/_2$ pint) coconut milk
2 tbsp Thai fish sauce
15 g ($^1/_2$ oz) palm sugar, grated
juice of $^1/_2$ lime

To garnish:
coriander leaves
sliced red chilli
finely chopped cashew nuts

boiled rice, to serve

Heat the oil in a wok or deep frying pan and stir-fry the onion, garlic and ginger for 1 minute. Add the beef and turmeric and stir-fry for a further 2–3 minutes until the beef is golden.

Add the cashew nuts, coconut milk, fish sauce, sugar and lime juice and cook for 2–3 minutes until thickened and the beef is tender. Garnish with coriander leaves, chilli and chopped cashew nuts and serve with plain boiled rice.

FILLET STEAK WITH BLUE CHEESE BUTTER

Serves: 4
Preparation time: 5 minutes, plus chilling
Cooking time: 6–12 minutes

Treat yourself and friends to a gorgeous fillet steak, cooked to your liking and topped with a piquant blue cheese butter. Make the butter up to 3 days ahead and keep refrigerated until required.

125 g (4 oz) butter, softened
50 g (2 oz) Roquefort cheese, crumbled
salt and pepper
4 x 250 g (8 oz) beef fillet steaks

To serve:
boiled new potatoes
green salad

Beat 75 g/3 oz of the butter, the cheese and a little pepper together. Wrap in a small piece of foil and chill for 30 minutes in the fridge. Remove from the fridge and cut into thick slices.

Season the steaks well with salt and pepper. Melt the remaining butter in a large frying pan and, as soon as it stops foaming, add the steaks. Fry over a medium heat for 3–4 minutes each side for rare, 4–5 minutes for medium and 6 minutes for well done. Wrap the steaks loosely in foil and rest for 5 minutes.

Serve the steaks topped with the butter, all the pan juices and the juices collected in the foil. Serve with new potatoes and a green salad.

THAI RED CURRY BEEF BURGER

Serves: 4
Preparation time: 5 minutes, plus chilling
Cooking time: 6–8 minutes

Thai red curry paste is readily available from the Asian section of your local supermarket. It makes a fiery addition to beef burgers – add more or less as required. Make and shape the burgers several hours ahead and keep chilled. Return to room temperature 1 hour before cooking.

750 g (1^{1}/$_{2}$ lb) minced beef
1–1^{1}/$_{2}$ tbsp Thai red curry paste
40 g (1^{1}/$_{2}$ oz) fresh white breadcrumbs
2 tbsp chopped fresh coriander
4 Kaffir lime leaves, very finely chopped
1 egg, lightly beaten
1 tbsp light soy sauce
pepper

To serve:
toasted sesame seed buns
shredded lettuce
sweet chilli sauce

49

Put the beef into a bowl and stir in the red curry paste, breadcrumbs, coriander, lime leaves, egg, soy sauce and some pepper. Using your hands mix together until sticky. Shape the mixture into 4 large burgers.

Cook the burgers on a barbecue or heated ridged grill pan for 4–5 minutes each side until charred and cooked through. Serve them in toasted buns with shredded lettuce and sweet chilli sauce.

BEEF AND GUINNESS PIE

Serves: 4
Preparation time: 25 minutes
Cooking time: 2^1/$_2$ hours

4 tbsp olive oil
1 onion, chopped
1 garlic clove, crushed
2 carrots, chopped
2 celery sticks, chopped
1 tbsp chopped fresh thyme
1 kg (2 lb) stewing steak, cubed
1 tbsp plain flour
salt and pepper
600 ml (1 pint) Guinness
1 x 400 g (13 oz) can chopped tomatoes
2 bay leaves
450 g (1 lb) puff pastry, thawed if frozen
1 egg, lightly beaten

Heat half the oil in a flameproof casserole and fry the onion, garlic, carrot, celery and thyme for 10 minutes until the vegetables are softened, then remove with a slotted spoon.

Place the meat in a bowl and add the flour and plenty of salt and pepper. Stir well to coat the meat evenly. Add the remaining oil to the pan and fry the beef for 4–5 minutes until browned. Return the vegetables to the pan, add the Guinness and stir well, scraping the sticky bits from the base of the pan. Add the tomatoes and bay leaves, bring to the boil, cover and simmer for 1–1^1/$_2$ hours or until the beef is tender. Discard the bay leaves and set aside to cool.

Preheat the oven to 200°C/400°F/Gas Mark 6 and grease a 2 litre/3^1/$_2$ pint pie dish. Roll out the pastry on a lightly floured surface to about 2.5 cm/1 in larger than the pie dish. Tip the stew into the dish, brush the rim with a little beaten egg and top with the pastry, pressing down well. Trim the excess pastry with a sharp knife and crimp the edges with a forefinger. Flute the pastry by tapping all the way round with a sharp knife.

Cut out leaf shapes from the pastry trimmings. Brush the pastry lid with beaten egg, arrange the leaves in a pattern over the top and brush these with egg. Pierce a small slit in the centre and bake for 35–40 minutes until the pastry is risen and golden.

STEAK WITH ASIAN-STYLE MUSHROOM SAUCE

Serves: 4
Preparation time: 10 minutes
Cooking time: 12–15 minutes

Rib eye is a delicious cut of steak and is a slightly cheaper option to fillet. Sirloin could also be used.

4 x 250 g (8 oz) rib eye beef steaks
salt and pepper
25 g (1 oz) butter
2 tbsp sunflower oil
2 garlic cloves, crushed
1 tsp grated root ginger
a pinch of Chinese five-spice powder
350 g (12 oz) mixed Asian mushrooms, such as oyster and
    shiitake
50 ml (2 fl oz) Chinese rice wine or dry sherry
150 ml ($^1/_4$ pint) fresh beef stock
2 tbsp dark soy sauce
2 tbsp chopped fresh parsley

Season the steaks with salt and pepper. Melt the butter in a frying pan and as soon as it stops foaming add the steaks and fry over a medium heat for 3–4 minutes side for rare, 4–5 minutes each side for medium and 6 minutes each side for well done. Wrap loosely in foil and leave to rest for 5 minutes.

Add the oil to the pan and stir-fry the garlic, ginger and Chinese five-spice for 30 seconds, then add the mushrooms and stir-fry over a high heat for 3–4 minutes until golden. Add the wine and reduce by half. Add the stock, soy sauce and the beef juices collected in the foil and simmer for 3–4 minutes until thickened. Sprinkle over the parsley and serve the steaks topped with the mushroom sauce.

CLASSIC LASAGNE

Serves: 4
Preparation time: 35 minutes, plus infusing
Cooking time: 1 hour

2 tbsp olive oil
1 onion, finely chopped
1 carrot, finely chopped
1 stick celery, finely chopped
2 garlic cloves, crushed
125 g (4 oz) smoked pancetta or bacon, diced
500 g (1 lb) minced beef
400 g (13 oz) can chopped tomatoes
150 ml ($^1/_4$ pint) red wine
4 tbsp tomato purée
2 tbsp chopped fresh basil
salt and pepper
250 g (8 oz) fresh lasagne sheets
50 g (2 oz) grated Parmesan cheese

Béchamel sauce:
1 onion, roughly chopped
2 bay leaves (or 1 dried)
2 cloves
600 ml (1 pint) milk
40 g (1$^1/_2$ oz) butter
40 g (1$^1/_2$ oz) plain flour

Heat the oil in a saucepan and gently fry the onion, carrot, celery, garlic and bacon for 5 minutes, then add the mince and fry for a further 5 minutes until brown, stirring frequently to break up the mince. Add the tomatoes, wine, tomato purée, basil and salt and pepper. Bring to the boil, cover and simmer for 30 minutes until thickened.

Preheat the oven to 200°C/400°F/Gas Mark 6. Meanwhile, make the béchamel sauce. Put the onion, bay leaves, cloves and milk into a saucepan with salt and pepper to taste. Bring to the boil, remove from the heat and set aside to infuse for 20 minutes and then strain. Melt the butter in a clean saucepan, add the flour and stir over a medium heat for 30 seconds. Gradually stir in the infused milk and continue to cook, stirring until the mixture boils. Cook for 2 minutes and remove from the heat.

Spoon a third of the tomato sauce into a square baking dish and top with a third of the lasagne sheets, a third of the béchamel and a third of the cheese. Repeat to make a further 2 layers, ending with the cheese. Bake for 30 minutes.

MUSTARD-CRUSTED BEEF ROAST

Serves: 4–6
Preparation time: 10 minutes
Cooking time: 1¹/₄ hours

There is nothing better than a good old-fashioned Sunday roast of beef, crispy roast potatoes and meltingly tender onions. Here the beef is coated with mustard and thyme for a slight variation.

> 750 g (1¹/₂ lb) main crop potatoes, such as Desirée,
>   quartered
> 4 onions, left whole
> 2 tbsp wholegrain mustard
> 2 tbsp chopped fresh thyme
> salt and pepper
> 1.5 kg (1¹/₂ lb) rolled sirloin of beef
> 4 tbsp olive oil
> 1 tbsp plain flour
> 150 ml (¹/₄ pint) red wine
> 300 ml (¹/₂ pint) beef stock
>
> 1 x quantity Yorkshire puddings (see page 134)

Preheat the oven to 220°C/425°F/Gas Mark 7. Put the potatoes and onions in a large saucepan of lightly salted water, bring to the boil and cook for 5 minutes. Drain well and return the potatoes to the pan. Shake the pan vigorously so that the potatoes become fluffy on the outside.

Mix the mustard and thyme with a little salt and pepper and spread all over the beef. Put the oil into a heavy-based roasting tin and place in the oven for 5 minutes. Add the potatoes and onions and cook for 15 minutes, then add the beef, nestling it amongst the potatoes. Roast for a further 45 minutes, turning the potatoes and onions every 15 minutes.

Wrap the beef loosely in foil and set aside to rest for 15 minutes. Transfer the onions and potatoes to a dish and keep warm.

Discard all but 1 tablespoon of the fat from the roasting tin, place on a gentle heat, stir in the flour and cook for 1 minute. Stir in the wine and cook for 3 minutes and then stir in the stock. Cook for a further 3–4 minutes until the gravy is thickened, and season to taste.

Carve the beef thinly and serve with the potatoes, onions and gravy and Yorkshire puddings.

PROVENCAL BEEF STEW

Serves: 4
Preparation time: 30 minutes, plus marinating overnight
Cooking time: 3 hours

A good tip for peeling baby onions with ease is to place them in a saucepan, cover with cold water and bring to the boil. Remove the onions, refresh under cold water and peel. The flavours of this stew improve with time, so it can be made up to 24 hours ahead. Once cold, store in the fridge and reheat over a medium heat for 20–30 minutes until bubbling.

1 kg (2 lb) stewing steak, cubed
2 tbsp olive oil
2 garlic cloves, crushed
1 tbsp chopped fresh thyme
450 ml ($3/4$ pint) red wine
250 g (8 oz) baby onions, peeled and left whole
2 carrots, thickly sliced
2 sticks celery, thickly sliced
4 strips orange peel
2 bay leaves
1 x 400 g (13 oz) can chopped tomatoes
4 tbsp tomato purée
300 ml ($1/2$ pint) beef stock
salt and pepper
4 anchovy fillets, drained and chopped
100 g (4 oz) pitted black olives
2 tbsp chopped fresh parsley

mashed potato, to serve

Place the beef in a large bowl with the olive oil, garlic, thyme and red wine, cover and marinate in the fridge overnight.

Place the beef and its marinade in a flameproof casserole and add the onions, carrots, celery, orange peel, bay leaves, tomatoes, tomato purée, stock and salt and pepper. Bring to the boil and cook, covered, over a very gentle heat for 2 hours.

Stir in the anchovies, olives and parsley and cook, uncovered, for a further 30 minutes–1 hour until the stew is thickened and the meat meltingly tender. Serve with mashed potato.

MEATBALLS WITH SPAGHETTI

Serves: 4
Preparation time: 20 minutes
Cooking time: 35 minutes

Wetting hands with cold water makes shaping meatballs and burgers far easier as it prevents the mixture from sticking to your hands. The meatballs and their sauce can be made ahead of time and heated through later on. Keep chilled and reheat over a medium heat for 20 minutes until the sauce and meatballs are hot.

4 tbsp extra virgin olive oil
1 onion, finely chopped
2 garlic cloves, crushed
2 tsp chopped rosemary
1 tsp ground cumin
750 g (1$^1/_2$ lb) ground minced lamb
50 g (2 oz) fresh white breadcrumbs
2 tbsp freshly grated Parmesan cheese
salt and pepper
120 ml (4 fl oz) dry white wine
1 x 400 g (13 oz) can chopped thick tomatoes
150 ml ($^1/_4$ pint) chicken stock
2 tbsp sun-dried tomato paste
500 g (1 lb) dried spaghetti

Heat half the oil in a frying pan and fry the onion, garlic, rosemary and cumin for 6–8 minutes until the onion is softened. Remove from the heat and leave to cool.

Mix together the mince, onion mixture, breadcrumbs, Parmesan, salt and pepper and, using your hands, work together until evenly combined. Using slightly wet hands, shape the mixture into 20 balls.

Heat the remaining oil in a large frying pan and fry the meatballs over a medium heat for 5 minutes until browned on all sides. Add the wine to the pan and bring to the boil. Cook for 2 minutes until reduced by about half. Add the tomatoes, stock, sun-dried tomato paste and pepper to taste and bring to the boil. Cover and cook for 20 minutes until the meatballs are cooked.

Cook the spaghetti according to the packet instructions until al dente (just cooked). Drain well and serve with the meatballs, sauce and extra Parmesan cheese.

LAMB WITH BEETROOT JAM AND AÏOLI

Serves: 4
Preparation time: 5 minutes
Cooking time: 20 minutes

Make the jam and aïoli in advance. Cover the aïoli with cling film and store both in the fridge. Return the jam to room temperature before serving.

3 tbsp extra virgin olive oil
1 red onion, sliced
250 g (8 oz) cooked beetroot in natural juices, diced
75 ml (3 fl oz) red wine
2 tbsp redcurrant jelly
2 tbsp balsamic vinegar
750 g (1 1/2 lb) lamb tenderloin
1 tbsp dried thyme
2 tsp sea salt
2 tsp crushed black pepper

Aïoli:
1 garlic clove, crushed
1 egg yolk
2 tsp lemon juice
1 tsp Dijon mustard
salt
150 ml (1/4 pint) olive oil

Make the aïoli: put the garlic, egg yolk, lemon juice, mustard and a little salt in a food processor and pulse briefly until frothy. With the blade running, add the oil in a steady stream through the funnel until the sauce is thick and glossy. Thin with a little boiling water if too thick.

Heat 2 tablespoons of the virgin oil in a saucepan and fry the onion for 10 minutes until softened. Add the beetroot and fry for a further 5 minutes. Stir in the wine, redcurrant jelly and vinegar and stir until the jelly is melted. Cook for 3–4 minutes until the sauce is thickened.

Heat a ridged grill pan until hot. Brush the lamb with the remaining oil and rub all over with the thyme, salt and pepper. Cook the lamb for 3 minutes each side. Wrap loosely in foil and leave to rest for 5 minutes.

Slice the lamb thickly and serve hot with the beetroot jam, aïoli and the juices collected in the foil.

INDIAN LAMB CURRY

Serves: 4
Preparation time: 25 minutes, plus marinating overnight
Cooking time: $1^1/_2$ hours

1 kg (2 lb) boneless leg of lamb
1 onion, sliced
500 g (1 lb) tomatoes, diced
450 ml ($^3/_4$ pint) water
2 tbsp sunflower oil
4 tbsp chopped fresh coriander

Marinade:
1 onion, roughly chopped
4 garlic cloves, roughly chopped
2 tsp grated root ginger
1 large red chilli, seeded and chopped
2 tsp ground coriander
1 tsp ground cumin
1 tsp ground turmeric
1 tsp salt
$^1/_2$ tsp ground cinnamon
$^1/_2$ tsp ground white pepper
2 tbsp red wine vinegar

To serve:
boiled basmati rice
naan bread
mango chutney

Cut the lamb into chunks, discarding any gristle and excess fat. Place in a large bowl.

Make the marinade: place all the ingredients in a food processor and process to form a smooth paste. Add to the lamb, stir well until evenly coated, cover and marinate in the fridge overnight.

Place the meat and all the marinade juices in a saucepan with the sliced onion, tomatoes, water and oil. Bring to the boil, cover and simmer gently for 1 hour. Remove the lid, stir in the coriander and cook, uncovered, for 15 minutes until the sauce is thickened. Adjust seasonings and serve with rice, naan bread and mango chutney.

MINTED LAMB STEAKS

Serves: 4
Preparation time: 10 minutes, plus marinating
Cooking time: 10 minutes

The mint and cumin butter can be made up to 3 days in advance and chilled until required.

> 4 x 250 g (8 oz) lamb leg steaks
> 2 tbsp extra virgin olive oil
> grated zest and juice of 1 unwaxed lemon
> 2 garlic cloves
> salt and pepper
>
> Mint and cumin butter:
> 2 tsp cumin seeds
> 125 g (4 oz) butter
> 2 tbsp chopped fresh mint
> a pinch of ground cayenne pepper

Make the butter: dry fry the cumin seeds in a small frying pan until browned, cool slightly and then grind to a fine powder in a spice grinder. Beat into the butter with the chopped mint and cayenne. Roll into a log shape and chill in the fridge until required. Slice thinly.

Place the lamb steaks in a shallow dish and add the oil, lemon zest and juice, garlic and salt and pepper to taste and rub well into the meat. Cover and marinate for 30 minutes.

Preheat the grill to high or a ridged grill pan until hot. Remove the lamb from its marinade and grill or griddle for 4–5 minutes each side. Rest for 5 minutes and then serve each steak topped with 2 slices of the mint and cumin butter.

LAMB AND PASTA BAKE

Serves: 4
Preparation time: 15 minutes
Cooking time: 1 hour

If you prefer, you can buy béchamel sauce ready-made from the chilled cabinet of your local supermarket, otherwise follow the recipe on page 53. This dish can be assembled ahead of time, ready for cooking later on. You may need to increase the cooking time by up to 15 minutes.

2 tbsp olive oil
1 onion, finely chopped
2 garlic cloves, crushed
2 tsp chopped fresh rosemary
500 g (1 lb) lamb mince
1 x 400 g (13 oz) can chopped tomatoes
2 tbsp tomato purée
salt and pepper
250 g (8 oz) dried penne
2 eggs, lightly beaten
50 g (2 oz) grated Parmesan cheese
1 quantity béchamel sauce (see above)

green salad, to serve

Heat the oil in a saucepan and gently fry the onion, garlic and rosemary for 5 minutes until the onion is softened. Increase the heat, add the mince and stir-fry for 5 minutes until browned. Add the tomatoes, tomato purée and salt and pepper. Bring to the boil, cover and simmer gently for 20 minutes.

Cook the pasta according to the packet instructions until al dente (just cooked). Drain well and return to the pan. Preheat the oven to 200°C/400°F/Gas Mark 6 and grease a 20x30 cm/8x12 in baking dish.

Stir the eggs and half of the Parmesan into the béchamel sauce.

Put half of the cooked pasta in the dish, top with half of the lamb sauce and half of the béchamel sauce. Repeat the layers and scatter over the remaining cheese. Bake for 30 minutes or until bubbling and golden. Cool for 15 minutes before serving with a green salad.

HERB-ROASTED LAMB RACKS

Serves: 4
Preparation time: 10 minutes
Cooking time: 20 minutes, plus marinating and resting

You will need 2 racks of lamb, both with 8 cutlets each.

2 garlic cloves, crushed
1 tbsp ground coriander
2 tbsp olive oil
grated zest of 1 lemon
1 tbsp chopped fresh rosemary
1 tbsp chopped fresh thyme
salt and black pepper
2 x 8 bone racks spring lamb (about 500 g/1 lb each)
6 sprigs of fresh rosemary

Tomato, olive and onion salad:
4 tomatoes, sliced
1/2 onion, sliced
50 g (2 oz) pitted black olives
salt and pepper
extra virgin olive oil
lemon juice

kitchen string

Preheat the oven to 200°C/400°F/Gas Mark 6. Combine the garlic, coriander, oil, lemon zest, herbs, salt and pepper, stir well and rub over the meat. Cover and leave to marinate for 30 minutes. Top the spice mix with rosemary sprigs and tie in place with the kitchen string.

Make the tomato, olive and onion salad: mix together the tomatoes, onion and olives. Season with salt and pepper and dress with extra virgin olive oil and a drizzle of lemon juice.

Place racks, fat side up on a rack set in a roasting tin, and cook for 20 minutes. Remove from the oven, cover with foil and leave to rest for 5 minutes. Remove the string and roesemary sprigs and slice the lamb into cutlets, allowing 4 per person. Serve with the tomato, olive and onion salad.

LAMB RACKS WITH LENTILS AND SPINACH

Serves: 4
Preparation time: 15 minutes
Cooking time: 1 hour, plus resting

250 g (8 oz) puy lentils
1 litre (1$^3/_4$ pint) chicken stock
2 garlic cloves, left whole
2 sprigs fresh thyme
250 g (8 oz) spinach leaves, washed and dried (500g/1lb bunch)
25 g (1 oz) butter
2 tsp chopped fresh thyme
1 tsp ground cumin
salt and pepper
2 x 8 rib lamb racks (see page 62)

Preheat the oven to 220°C/425°F/Gas Mark 7. Put the lentils into a saucepan with the stock, garlic and thyme sprigs. Bring to the boil and simmer gently over a low heat for 30–35 minutes until the lentils are cooked and the stock absorbed. Discard the thyme and stir in the spinach and butter. Cook for a further 5 minutes until the spinach is wilted. Keep warm.

Combine the oil, chopped thyme, cumin and salt and pepper in a bowl. Rub the mixture all over the lamb racks and place in a roasting tin fat-side up. Roast for 20 minutes, remove from the oven, cover loosely with foil and set aside to rest for 10 minutes.

Cut each rack in half to give each person 4 cutlets and serve with the lentils and spinach.

GRILLED LAMB CUTLETS WITH TABBOULEH

Serves: 2
Preparation time: 20 minutes, plus marinating
Cooking time: 6-8 minutes

Tabbouleh is the name of a Middle Eastern salad made with bulghar wheat and lots of fresh chopped herbs, garlic and tomatoes. It makes a lovely accompaniment to grilled meats and fish.

6 lamb cutlets
1 tbsp extra virgin olive oil
grated zest and juice 1 unwaxed lemon
2 tsp chopped fresh rosemary
2 garlic cloves, crushed
$1/2$ tsp ground cinnamon
salt and pepper

Tabbouleh:
50 g (2 oz) bulghar wheat
juice of $1/2$ lemon juice
75 ml (3 fl oz) extra virgin olive oil
1 bunch flat leaf parley, finely chopped
$1/2$ bunch fresh mint, finely chopped
4 spring onions, finely chopped

Greek yogurt, to serve

Place the lamb cutlets in a shallow dish, and add the oil, lemon zest and juice, rosemary, garlic, cinnamon, salt and pepper and rub well together to coat the lamb. Leave to marinate until required.

Make the tabbouleh: soak the bulghar wheat in plenty of cold water for 10 minutes, drain well and place in a bowl. Add the lemon juice and olive oil and leave to soak for 30 minutes. Stir in the herbs, onions and some salt and pepper and set aside while cooking the lamb.

Heat a ridged grill pan until hot and cook the lamb for 2-3 minutes each side until cooked through. Serve with the tabbouleh and Greek yogurt.

FISH AND SEAFOOD

You can add variety to your fish dishes with seafood like mussels and squid (not shown). The other fresh ingredients that you will need to make any of the fish recipes are highlighted in the fridge. Extra ingredients or vegetables to serve are shown on the list. Always read through the recipe you choose to make sure that you have all the ingredients to hand.

DRY CIDER
SMOKED BACON
RED ONION
ONION
FRENCH BEANS
POTATOES
NEW POTATOES
SUGAR SNAP PEAS
MIXED CHOPPED FRESH HERBS
FRESH CHIVES
FRESH SAGE
THAI BASIL LEAVES
LEMONGRASS
FRESH ROOT GINGER
PEACHES OR NECTARINES
FRESH BAY LEAVES
KAFFIR LIME LEAVES
SAFFRON STRANDS
FRESH ROOT GINGER
DRIED RED CHILLI FLAKES
CHINESE FIVE-SPICE POWDER
SQUID TUBES
SMOKED SALMON
VERMICELLI RICE NOODLES
DRIED SPAGHETTI
THAI FISH SAUCE
HOISIN SAUCE
DARK SOY SAUCE
SESAME OIL
DRY WHITE WINE
CHUNKY BREAD
BURGER BUNS
BAGUETTES
DIJON MUSTARD
CREAMED HORSERADISH
MAYONNAISE
CORNFLOUR
CAPERS IN BRINE
ANCHOVY FILLETS
BLACK OLIVES
GREEN OLIVES
RED WINE VINEGAR
BALSAMIC VINEGAR
WHITE WINE VINEGAR
HAZELNUT OIL
DIJON MUSTARD
HAZELNUTS
ARBORIO RICE
CREAM CHEESE

MUSSELS COOKED IN CIDER

Serves: 4
Preparation time: 10 minutes
Cooking time: 6–7 minutes

Mussels are ideal when entertaining on a budget, as they are really inexpensive and go a long way. Look out for farmed mussels which tend to be far cleaner and are available year round.

> 1 kg (2 lb) mussels
> 1 onion, chopped
> 1 garlic clove, crushed
> 1 stick celery, chopped
> 100 ml (3 $^1/_2$ fl oz) dry cider
> salt and pepper
> 50 ml (2 fl oz) single cream
> 1 tbsp chopped fresh parsley
> 1 tbsp chopped celery leaves
>
> French bread, to serve

Wash the mussels under cold running water, scrubbing the shells clean and pulling off any scraggly 'beards' still attached to the shells.

Put the onions, garlic, celery and cider in a large saucepan and bring to the boil. Add the mussels, cover and cook over a medium heat for 4–5 minutes until all the shells have opened (discard any that remain closed).

Strain the mussels through a colander and place in a large bowl, cover with foil and place in a very low oven to keep warm. Strain the juices through a fine sieve into a clean pan and bring to the boil, whisk in the cream and simmer for a few minutes until thickened slightly. Season to taste.

Pour the liquid over the mussels, scatter over the herbs and serve immediately with plenty of crusty French bread to mop up the juices.

ROASTED MULLET WITH POTATOES AND BACON

Serves: 4
Preparation time: 20 minutes
Cooking time: 35–40 minutes

Ask your fishmonger to fillet 4 large red mullet for you. You could use bream, trout or sea bass fillets instead.

> 500 g (1 lb) waxy potatoes, such as
>   King Edward or Desirée
> 125 g (4 oz) smoked bacon, diced
> 1 large red onion, thickly sliced
> 4 garlic cloves, sliced
> 1 tbsp chopped fresh thyme
> 1 tbsp chopped fresh sage
> salt and pepper
> 3 tbsp extra virgin olive oil
> 8 x 75 g (3 oz) red mullet fillets
>
> Salsa verde, to serve (see page 80)

Preheat the oven to 220°C/425°F/Gas Mark 7. Combine the potatoes, bacon, onion, garlic, herbs and salt and pepper to taste with 2 tablespoons of the oil in a roasting tin and stir well. Roast for 30 minutes.

Season the mullet fillets with salt and pepper. Remove the roasting tin from the oven and arrange the fish, skin-side up over the top. Drizzle over the remaining oil and return to the oven for a further 6–8 minutes until the fish and vegetables are cooked.

Serve at once with salsa verde.

HOT AND SOUR SEAFOOD SOUP

Serves: 4
Preparation time: 20 minutes
Cooking time: 25 minutes

To cook vermicelli rice noodles, follow the instructions on the packet as brands vary. The noodles can be cooked ahead of time and warmed through just prior to serving – place cooked noodles in a sieve and pour over boiling water, shake dry and transfer to serving bowls.

12 raw tiger prawns, peeled and de-veined (see page 84)
2 stalks lemongrass, chopped
6 large Kaffir lime leaves, torn
5 cm (2 in) piece of root ginger, sliced
4 garlic cloves, roughly chopped
350 g (12 oz) white fish fillet, such as cod
350 g (12 oz) prepared squid tubes
100 ml (3 $^{1}/_{2}$ fl oz) Thai fish sauce
100 ml (3 $^{1}/_{2}$ fl oz) lime juice
2 tbsp caster sugar
2 red bird's-eye chillies, thinly sliced
1 bunch coriander leaves, chopped

vermicelli rice noodles, to serve

Peel and de-vein the prawns and place the heads and shells in a saucepan with the lemongrass, lime leaves, ginger, garlic and 1.5 litres/ 3 pints of cold water. Bring to the boil and simmer gently for 20 minutes. Strain the stock into a clean pan and return to the heat.

Prepare the seafood: cut the fish into chunks. Cut the squid tubes in half lengthways and open out flat, using a sharp knife score the inside with a diamond pattern and then cut each into 6 pieces.

Add the prawns and fish to the hot stock and cook for 1 minute. Add the squid, fish sauce, lime juice and sugar and cook for a further 1–2 minutes until the seafood is cooked.

Pour the fish mixture over the noodles and serve topped with the chillies and coriander leaves.

SPAGHETTI VONGOLE

Serves: 4
Preparation time: 10 minutes
Cooking time: 15 minutes

Small clams or vongole are perfect tossed with pasta, garlic and chilli.
If you can't find clams, this dish tastes just as good with mussels. Simply
substitute clams with an equal quantity of mussels and follow the same
method.

1 kg (2 lb) small clams
500 g (1 lb) dried spaghetti
6 tbsp extra virgin olive oil
4 garlic cloves, crushed
a pinch of dried red chilli flakes
grated zest and juice of 1 unwaxed lemon
150 ml ($^1/_4$ pint) dry white wine
2 tbsp chopped fresh parsley
salt and pepper

chunky bread, to serve

Wash the clams in cold water, scrubbing any dirt from the shells, and
shake dry. Cook the pasta according to the packet instructions until al dente
(just cooked). Drain well and return to the pan.

Heat the oil in a large saucepan and gently fry the garlic, chilli, lemon
zest and salt and pepper (to taste) for 5 minutes until soft but not browned.
Add the wine and boil until reduced by half. Add the clams and cook, covered,
for 5 minutes, shaking the pan from time to time until all the shells have
opened (discard any that remain closed).

Stir in the lemon juice, parsley and cooked pasta and stir over a
medium heat for 1 minute. Serve hot with bread to mop up the juices.

POACHED SALMON WITH HERB MAYONNAISE

Serves: 4
Preparation time: 5 minutes
Cooking: 5 minutes, plus cooling

Making mayonnaise by hand is just as simple as in the food processor: just remember to add the oil slowly, beating well between each addition. If making ahead of time, place the mayonnaise in a bowl and cover the surface with cling film. Chill until required.

> 4 x 250 g (8 oz) salmon
> $^1/_2$ lemon, sliced
> a few sprigs of fresh tarragon and parsley
> 2 bay leaves
> salt and pepper
>
> Herb mayonnaise:
> 1 egg yolk
> 1 tsp Dijon mustard
> 1 tsp lemon juice
> 150 ml ($^1/_4$ pint) olive oil
> 2 tbsp chopped fresh herbs, to include basil,
>   parsley and tarragon
>
> boiled new potatoes, to serve

Pull out any small bones from the salmon fillets with a pair of tweezers and lay the salmon skin-side up in a frying pan. Add enough water just to cover the fish and add the lemon slices, herbs, bay leaves and salt and pepper to taste. Bring the pan to the boil, cook for 5 minutes and remove the salmon from the pan. Set aside to cool completely.

Make the herb mayonnaise: place the egg yolk, mustard, lemon juice and salt in the food processor and mix briefly until frothy. Then, with the motor running, gradually pour in the oil through the funnel until the sauce is thick and glossy. If necessary, thin with a little boiling water. Add the herbs and process briefly until the sauce is flecked green.

Serve the cold salmon with new potatoes and a dollop of the herb mayonnaise.

BARBECUED HOISIN SALMON

Serves: 4
Preparation time: 5 minutes, plus marinating
Cooking time: 6 minutes

There are several brands of hoisin sauce available from your supermarket, but I recommend a trip to your nearest Asian food store to buy a more authentic brand – it will be a fascinating experience as Asian food stores sell a wonderful selection of unusual ingredients.

4 x 250 g (8 oz) salmon steaks
2 tbsp hoisin sauce
2 tbsp dark soy sauce
1 tsp sesame oil
$1/4$ tsp Chinese five-spice powder
1 garlic clove, crushed
1 tsp grated root ginger

green salad, to serve

Place the salmon steaks in a shallow dish. Combine the remaining ingredients, add to the salmon and toss well until evenly coated. Marinate for 30 minutes.

Preheat the grill to high and cook the fish steaks for 3 minutes each side until charred and cooked through, basting with the marinade. Rest for 3 minutes and serve with a green salad.

SMOKED SALMON AND POTATO TART

Serves: 4–6
Preparation time: 5 minutes
Cooking time: 1–1¹/₄ hours

This tasty smoked salmon and potato tart is just as good cold as hot and makes great picnic food.

2 tbsp extra virgin olive oil, plus extra for greasing
250 g (8 oz) ricotta
1 garlic clove, crushed
2 tbsp chopped fresh dill
750 g (1 lb) main crop potatoes, such as Desirée or
    King Edward's
pepper
350 g (12 oz) smoked salmon
6 tomatoes, thinly sliced

Preheat the oven to 220°C/425°F/Gas Mark 7 and use a little of the oil to grease a 23 cm/9 in loose-bottom cake tin. Combine the ricotta, garlic and dill in a bowl.

Slice the potatoes as thinly as possible and arrange a layer over the base of the prepared tin. Season with pepper and top with a layer of salmon. Carefully spread the salmon with a third of the ricotta mixture and top with tomato slices. Repeat the layers, finishing with a layer of potatoes.

Brush over the remaining oil and bake for 1–1¹/₄ hours until a skewer inserted in the middle comes out hot to the touch (cover the tin with foil if it starts to brown too much). Remove from the oven, rest for 5 minutes and then turn out and serve cut into wedges, or leave to go cold.

SALMON AND SWEET POTATO CAKES WITH LIME AÏOLI

Serves: 4
Preparation time: 20 minutes
Cooking time: 20 minutes, plus cooling

500 g (1 lb) salmon fillets
salt and pepper
500 g (1 lb) sweet potatoes, cubed
4 spring onions, finely chopped
2 tbsp chopped fresh coriander
1 green chilli, deseeded and finely chopped
grated zest and juice of 1 lime
2 eggs, lightly beaten
4 tbsp seasoned plain flour
75 g (3 oz) dried breadcrumbs

Lime aïoli:
1 quantity aïoli (see page 58)
grated zest and juice of 1 lime

sunflower oil, for shallow frying
green salad, to serve

Place the salmon fillets in a frying pan, cover with cold water and add a little salt and pepper. Bring to the boil, simmer for 1 minute and then remove from the heat. Leave the fish to go cold in the pan, then flake into large pieces, discarding any bones.

Steam the sweet potatoes over a pan of simmering water for 10–15 minutes until tender. Transfer to a bowl and mash lightly with a fork. Leave to go cold.

Make the aïoli: combine the ingredients in a bowl and season to taste.

Combine the salmon, potato, spring onions, coriander, green chilli, lime zest and juice and salt and pepper to taste in a bowl and work together until combined. Shape the mixture into 8 cakes. Dip the cakes into the beaten egg, then into the flour and finally the breadcrumbs until evenly coated.

Heat a shallow layer of sunflower oil in a frying pan and fry the fish cakes for 3–4 minutes each side until crisp and golden. Serve the fish cakes with the aïoli and a green salad.

SEAFOOD PAELLA

Serves: 4
Preparation time: 20 minutes
Cooking time: 40 minutes, plus resting

Paella is similar to a risotto and is the national dish of Spain. It is essential to use arborio rice.

500 g (1 lb) small mussels (or clams)
12 raw tiger prawns
250 g (8 oz) swordfish fillet
250 g (8 oz) prepared squid tubes
a good pinch of saffron strands
600 ml (1 pint) hot fish stock
4 tbsp extra virgin olive oil
1 onion, chopped
2 garlic cloves, chopped
2 tsp ground paprika
1 x 400 g (13 oz) can chopped tomatoes
150 ml (¼ pint) white wine
300 g (10 oz) arborio rice
salt and pepper
2 tbsp chopped fresh parsley

Prepare the seafood: scrub the mussels (or clams), wash and dry well. Using a small pair of scissors, snip along the back of each prawn and carefully remove the intestinal tract. Wash and dry the prawns. Cut the swordfish into large chunks and the squid into thick rings.

Soak the saffron in the hot stock until required. Heat the oil in a large frying pan or paella pan and gently fry the onion, garlic and paprika for 10 minutes. Add the tomatoes and wine and bring to the boil. Scatter the rice over the pan and cook for 5 minutes without stirring.

Add three-quarters of the stock, stir once and cook over a gentle heat for 15 minutes. Stir in the remaining stock, mussels (or clams) and prawns and cook for 5 minutes, then add the swordfish and squid, stir well and cook for a further 5 minutes until the seafood is cooked and the stock absorbed (discard any mussels or clams that remain closed). Season to taste.

Scatter over the parsley, remove the pan from the heat, and cover with a clean tea towel. Leave to rest for 10 minutes, and serve hot.

SEARED TUNA NICOISE SALAD

Serves: 4
Preparation time: 20 minutes
Cooking time: 15 minutes

500 g (1 lb) new potatoes
250 g (8 oz) French beans
1 red onion, thinly sliced
2 tbsp capers, drained and washed
4 tomatoes, diced
125 g (4 oz) black olives
a handful of fresh basil leaves
4 x 200 g (7 oz) tuna steaks

Dressing:
100 ml (3$^{1}/_{2}$ fl oz) extra virgin olive oil
1$^{1}/_{2}$ tbsp red wine vinegar
1 garlic clove, crushed
salt and pepper

hard-boiled egg quarters, to serve

Boil the potatoes for 12–15 minutes until cooked, drain and place in a bowl. Meanwhile, make the dressing. Whisk the ingredients together until combined. Pour half over the potatoes, stir well and set aside to marinate.

Blanch the beans in lightly salted, boiling water for 2–3 minutes until just cooked, drain, refresh under cold water and pat dry.

Combine the potatoes, beans, onion, capers, tomatoes, olives, basil leaves and the remaining dressing. Stir well and set aside.

Rub the tuna steaks with a little oil and season with salt and pepper. Heat a ridged grill pan until hot, add the steaks and cook for 1 minute each side. Rest briefly and serve the tuna with the salad.

TUNA WITH ROASTED TOMATOES AND SALSA VERDE

Serves: 4
Preparation time: 15 minutes
Cooking time: 20 minutes

Make the salsa up to 48 hours ahead of time and store in the fridge in an airtight container until required.

500 g (1 lb) cherry tomatoes on the vine
2 tbsp extra virgin olive oil, plus extra for brushing
salt and pepper
1 tbsp balsamic vinegar
4 x 250 g (8 oz) tuna steaks

Salsa verde:
25 g (1 oz) parsley leaves
15 g ($^1/_2$ oz) mixed fresh herbs, such as basil, chives, mint
1 garlic clove, chopped
15 g ($^1/_2$ oz) pitted green olives
1 tbsp capers, drained and washed
2 anchovy fillets, washed and chopped
1 tsp Dijon mustard
2 tsp white wine vinegar
125 ml (4 fl oz) extra virgin olive oil

Preheat the oven to 220°C/425°F/Gas Mark 7. Place the cherry tomatoes still attached to the vine in a roasting tin, drizzle over the oil, season with salt and pepper and roast for 15 minutes. Drizzle over the vinegar and roast for a further 5 minutes until the tomatoes are softened. Remove from the oven and keep warm.

Make the salsa verde. Put all the ingredients in a food processor and process to form a thick paste. Season to taste and transfer to a bowl.

Heat a ridged grill pan until hot. Brush the tuna with oil, season liberally with salt and pepper and cook for 1 minute each side, rest for 3 minutes and serve with the tomatoes and salsa verde.

SWORDFISH BURGERS WITH CHILLI PEPPER SAUCE

Serves: 4
Preparation time: 15 minutes, plus marinating
Cooking time: 13 minutes

The chilli pepper sauce can be made up to 24 hours ahead. Store in the fridge until required.

4 x 200 g (7 oz) swordfish steaks
1 tbsp extra virgin olive oil
grated zest and juice of 1 unwaxed lemon
2 tsp chopped fresh thyme
salt and pepper
4 burger buns, halved and toasted
shredded lettuce leaves
mayonnaise

Chilli pepper sauce:
1 large red pepper
1 large red chilli
1 tbsp extra virgin olive oil
$^1/_2$ tbsp balsamic vinegar

Brush the swordfish fillets with a little oil and rub all over with the lemon zest, thyme and salt and pepper. Marinate for 30 minutes.

Make the chilli pepper sauce: preheat the grill to high and cook the pepper and chilli for 10 minutes, turning frequently until charred on all sides. Transfer to a plastic bag and set aside until cool enough to handle. Peel the pepper and chilli and discard the seeds, then chop the flesh. Place in a food processor with the oil, vinegar, salt and pepper to taste and process until really smooth.

Heat a ridged grill pan until hot and cook the swordfish fillets for 1–2 minutes each side until cooked. Squeeze over the lemon juice.

Fill each burger bun with the swordfish, shredded lettuce, mayonnaise and a spoonful of pepper sauce.

GARLIC PRAWN BAGUETTES

Serves: 4
Preparation time: 5 minutes
Cooking time: 5 minutes

> 50 g (2 oz) butter
> 500 g (1 lb) peeled raw prawns
> 2 garlic cloves, crushed
> 1 tbsp chopped fresh parsley
> juice of $\frac{1}{2}$ lemon
> salt and pepper
> 2 little gem lettuce
> 2 medium baguettes
>
> 1 x quantity Herb mayonnaise, to serve (see page 73)

Melt the butter in a large frying pan and, as soon as it stops foaming, add the prawns and garlic and cook over a medium heat for 4–5 minutes until the prawns are cooked through. Remove the pan from the heat and add the parsley, lemon juice and salt and pepper to taste.

Separate the lettuce leaves, and wash and dry them thoroughly. Stuff the leaves into the baguettes and spoon in the garlic prawns with all the pan juices. Serve hot with herb mayonnaise.

PRAWN, PEACH AND AVOCADO SALAD

Serves: 4
Preparation time: 20 minutes

De-veining prawns is the same for both cooked and raw prawns. Basically you are removing the intestinal tract that runs down the length of the prawn's back, which can be unpleasant if left in.

20 large cooked prawns
1 avocado, peeled, stoned and diced
2 peaches or nectarines, stoned and sliced
250 g (8 oz) cherry tomatoes
50 g (2 oz) hazelnuts, toasted
2 little gem lettuces, separated
a handful of fresh basil leaves, torn

Dressing:
1 tbsp white wine vinegar
2 tsp Dijon mustard
1 tsp caster sugar
4 tbsp hazelnut oil
2 tbsp extra virgin olive oil
salt and pepper

Peel the prawns and de-vein by cutting a slit along the back of each one, then pull out and discard the black intestinal tract. Wash the prawns and dry well on kitchen paper. Place the prawns in a large bowl with the avocado, peach slices, tomatoes, nuts, lettuce and basil leaves. Mix well.

Place the dressing ingredients in a screwtop jar and shake well until well combined. Pour the dressing over the salad and toss until evenly coated. Serve at once.

SMOKED HADDOCK AND PRAWN PIE

Serves: 4
Preparation time: 20 minutes
Cooking time: 40 minutes

250 g (8 oz) smoked haddock fillet
250 g (8 oz) cod fillet
300 ml (½ pint) milk
1 bay leaf
salt and pepper
25 g (1 oz) butter
1 onion, finely chopped
2 tsp chopped fresh thyme
40 g (1½ oz) plain flour
175 g (6 oz) cooked peeled prawns
2 tbsp chopped fresh parsley

Potato topping:
750 g (1½ lb) main crop potatoes, such as Desirée or
    King Edward's
50 g (2 oz) butter
50 g (2 oz) Cheddar cheese, grated

Preheat the oven to 200°C/400°F/Gas Mark 6 and grease a
23 cm/9 in square baking dish. Put the smoked haddock and cod in a
small frying pan, and add the milk, bay leaf and a little salt and pepper.
Bring to the boil and simmer gently, partially covered for 5 minutes. Remove
the fish from the milk, discard any skin and bones and flake the fish into
chunks. Strain the milk into a jug.

Melt the butter in a saucepan and gently fry the onion and thyme for
5 minutes until softened. Stir in the flour and cook for 30 seconds. Remove
the pan from the heat and stir in the reserved milk, return to the heat and
cook, stirring, until the sauce thickens. Simmer gently for 5 minutes then
remove from the heat. Carefully stir in the cooked fish, prawns and parsley
and season to taste. Spoon into the prepared dish.

Make the potato topping: cube the potatoes and boil for 10–15
minutes until tender. Drain well, return the potatoes to the pan and mash
with the butter, cheese and salt and pepper. Carefully spread the potato
mixture over the fish and fluff up the surface with a fork. Bake for 30–35
minutes until bubbling and golden. Cool for 10 minutes before serving.

POTTED SMOKED TROUT

Serves: 4
Preparation time: 10 minutes
Chilling time: 1 hour

This makes a great starter for a dinner party, it is rich, tasty and really simple to prepare ahead of time. This can be made up to 24 hours in advance of time and chilled until required. Serve straight from the fridge.

> 250 g (8 oz) smoked trout fillet, skinned
> 75 g (3 oz) unsalted butter, softened
> grated rind and juice $\frac{1}{2}$ orange
> 125 g (4 oz) cream cheese
> 2 tbsp creamed horseradish
> 1 tbsp chopped fresh chives
> pepper
>
> French bread, to serve

Flake the trout fillet and place in a food processor with 25 g/1 oz of the butter and all the remaining ingredients. Process until smooth, and season to taste.

Spoon the pâté into 4 x 150 ml/$\frac{1}{2}$ pint ramekin dishes and smooth flat. Chill for 30 minutes.

Melt the remaining butter in a small saucepan, carefully pour over the surface of the pâté and chill for a further 30 minutes or until set. Serve with crusty French bread.

SMOKED HADDOCK RISOTTO WITH SAGE BUTTER

Serves: 4
Preparation time: 20 minutes
Cooking time: 45–50 minutes

Arborio rice is a medium-grain or risotto rice. It is important to use this type of rice for a risotto. It should retain a slight bite when cooked.

500 g (1 lb) skinless smoked haddock fillet
600 ml (1 pint) milk
2 bay leaves
125 g (4 oz) butter
1 onion, finely chopped
2 garlic cloves, crushed
1 tbsp chopped fresh sage
300 g (10 oz) arborio rice
150 ml ($\frac{1}{4}$ pint) dry white wine
salt and pepper
20 sage leaves

Wash and dry the fish and pull out any remaining bones. Place in a large frying pan with the milk and bay leaves. Bring slowly to the boil, then simmer gently for 5 minutes. Lift out the fish, flake into large pieces and set aside. Strain the liquid into a jug and make up to 1.2 litre/2 pints with water and transfer to a saucepan. Bring to a very gentle simmer.

Melt half the butter in a separate saucepan and fry the onion, garlic and chopped sage for 5 minutes until softened but not brown. Add the rice and stir-fry for 1 minute until all the grains are glossy. Pour in the wine and boil rapidly for 3 minutes until absorbed.

Add a ladleful of the hot stock to the rice and stir until absorbed. Continue adding the stock and stirring the rice for about 20 minutes until the rice is tender and all the liquid is absorbed. Add the flaked fish and salt and pepper to taste. Stir well and remove from the heat. Leave to stand for 5 minutes.

Heat the remaining butter in a frying pan and fry the sage leaves for 1 minute until crispy and butter golden. Spoon the risotto into bowls and top each with the butter and sage leaves.

STIR-FRIED MONKFISH WITH THAI BASIL

Serves: 4
Preparation time: 10 minutes
Cooking time: 8 minutes

If possible, use Thai basil for this dish, which has a distinctive aniseed flavour. It is available from larger supermarkets or Asian food stores.

500 g (1 lb) monkfish, cubed
1 tbsp cornflour
$\frac{1}{4}$ tsp salt
2 tbsp sunflower oil
200 g (7 oz) sugar snaps
3 garlic cloves, crushed
2 bird's-eye red chillies, seeded and finely chopped
1$\frac{1}{2}$ tbsp Thai fish sauce
1$\frac{1}{2}$ tbsp light soy sauce
2 tbsp caster sugar
3 tbsp water
40 basil leaves, preferably Thai

boiled rice, to serve

Mix the fish with the cornflour and salt until evenly coated. Heat the oil in a frying pan and fry the fish pieces for 3 minutes until browned. Remove from the pan with a slotted spoon and set aside. Blanch the sugar snaps in lightly salted boiling water for 2 minutes until tender. Drain, refresh under cold water and pat dry, then set aside.

Return the pan to the heat and stir-fry the garlic and chillies over a low heat for 1 minute. Do not allow to burn. Add the fish sauce, soy sauce, sugar and water and cook for 30 seconds (do not allow the garlic to burn). Return the fish to the pan, add the sugar snaps and basil leaves and cook for 1–2 minutes until heated through. Serve with boiled rice.

VEGETABLES

You can make any of the vegetable dishes below from your weekly shop and your basic store cupboard. Most of the fresh ingredients are highlighted in the fridge. Any extra seasonings and side dishes to serve are listed here.

POTATOES
NEW POTATOES
CHINESE CABBAGE
CELERIAC
GREEN BEANS
FRESH ROOT GINGER
KAFFIR LIME LEAVES
FROZEN PEAS
GROUND CORIANDER
GROUND CUMIN
GROUND GINGER
CANNED CHICKPEAS
CANNED RED KIDNEY BEANS
CANNED CHOPPED TOMATOES
SEMI-DRIED TOMATOES
DRIED PORCINI
PASSATA
CRUSTY BREAD
PITTA BREAD
HOT CHILLI SAUCE
HOT CHILLI POWDER
DRIED RED CHILLI FLAKES
MEDIUM CURRY PASTE
THAI RED CURRY PASTE
MISO PASTE
TAHINI PASTE
STAR ANISE
LIGHT SOY SAUCE
DARK SOY SAUCE
FISH SAUCE
SESAME OIL
SUNFLOWER OIL
SMOKED TOFU
TOFU
RICE WINE VINEGAR
DRIED UDON NOODLES
COCONUT MILK
CORNFLOUR
BULGHAR WHEAT
PENNE
ORRECHIETTE
HAZELNUTS
PINE NUTS
SULTANAS
CAPERS

CELERIAC, APPLE AND STILTON SOUP

Serves: 4
Preparation time: 20 minutes
Cooking time: 30 minutes

Soup keeps well for up to 48 hours in the fridge or make in advance and freeze until needed.

25 g (1 oz) butter
1 onion, finely chopped
1 garlic clove, crushed
2 tsp chopped fresh thyme
500 g (1 lb) celeriac (peeled weight), diced
2 apples, peeled, cored and diced
1 litre (1³/₄ pints) vegetable stock
salt and pepper
100 g (3¹/₂ oz) Stilton, crumbled

Melt the butter in a saucepan and gently fry the onion, garlic and thyme for 5 minutes until the onions are softened. Add the celeriac and apples and fry gently for a further 5 minutes. Add the stock and salt and pepper to taste, bring to the boil, cover and simmer gently for 20 minutes until the celeriac is cooked.

Transfer the soup to a liquidizer, add the Stilton and blend until really smooth. Return the soup to the pan, heat through and serve at once.

MUSHROOM, MISO AND UDON NOODLE SOUP

Serves: 4
Preparation time: 10 minutes
Cooking time: 10 minutes

Miso paste is made from fermented soy beans and is used widely in Japanese cooking to flavour soups. Udon noodles are also Japanese: both are available from good quality healthfood stores.

1.5 litres (2$\frac{1}{2}$ pints) water
3 tbsp miso paste
4 tbsp dark soy sauce
2 tbsp sunflower oil
500 g (1 lb) mixed mushrooms, such as button, shiitake and oyster
250 g (8 oz) dried udon noodles

coriander leaves, to garnish

Whisk the water, miso paste and soy sauce together until smooth and place in a large saucepan. Heat gently until boiling.

Heat the oil in a saucepan and gently stir-fry the mushrooms for 5 minutes. Add to the stock and simmer gently for 5 minutes.

Cook the noodles according to the packet instructions and divide between 4 soup bowls. Pour over the mushroom soup and serve garnished with coriander leaves.

GRILLED PEPPER AND TOMATO SOUP WITH AÏOLI

Serves: 4
Preparation time: 15 minutes
Cooking time: 45 minutes

The garlicky aïoli is the perfect foil for this intensely flavoured pepper soup. This soup can be made up to 2 days ahead, or several days if frozen.

3 red peppers
2 tbsp olive oil
1 onion, finely chopped
2 garlic cloves, crushed
500 g (1 lb) ripe tomatoes, diced
900 ml (1$1/2$ pints) vegetable stock
2 tbsp chopped fresh basil
salt and pepper

1 x quantity Aïoli, to serve (see page 58)

Preheat the grill to high. Grill the peppers for 10 minutes, turning several times until the skins are evenly blackened. Place the peppers in a bowl, cover with cling film and set aside until cool enough to handle. Peel and discard the skin and seeds, cut the flesh into large dice.

Heat the oil in a saucepan and gently fry the onion and garlic for 10 minutes until the onion is softened. Add the tomatoes, stock, grilled pepper and some salt and pepper and bring to the boil. Cover and simmer gently for 20 minutes.

Transfer the soup to a liquidizer, add the basil and blend until the soup is really smooth. Return to the pan, adjust seasonings and heat through. Serve the soup topped with a swirl aioli.

CURRIED POTATO SALAD

Serves: 4
Preparation time: 5 minutes
Cooking time: 20 minutes

750 g (1^1/$_2$ lb) new potatoes
1 tbsp olive oil
1 small onion, sliced
1 garlic clove, crushed
2 tsp medium curry paste
150 g (5 oz) Greek–style natural yogurt
2 tbsp lemon juice
2 tbsp chopped fresh coriander
salt and pepper

Boil the new potatoes for 10–15 minutes until tender. Drain well, refresh briefly under cold water, drain again and transfer to a large bowl.

Heat the oil in a frying pan and gently fry the onion, garlic and curry paste for 10 minutes until the onion is softened. Stir the mixture into the potatoes.

Mix together the remaining ingredients, add to the potatoes and stir well until evenly combined. Season to taste and leave to cool.

TOMATO SALAD WITH BOCCONCINI

Serves: 4
Preparation time: 5 minutes, plus infusing

4 plum tomatoes, sliced
250 g (8 oz) red and yellow cherry tomatoes, halved
125 g (4 oz) semi-dried tomatoes
150 g (5 oz) bocconcini (mini mozzarella) balls, halved
1 garlic clove, crushed
grated zest of ^{1}/$_2$ unwaxed lemon
6 tbsp extra virgin olive oil
2 tbsp roughly chopped fresh coriander
salt and pepper

Arrange the tomatoes and bocconcini on a large platter. Combine the remaining ingredients and drizzle over the salad. Infuse for 30 minutes.

ASIAN VEGETABLE AND TOFU SALAD

Serves: 4
Preparation time: 15 minutes
Cooking time: 3 minutes

You could substitute marinated tofu for the smoked tofu, if preferred.

1 carrot
1 small cucumber
125 g (4 oz) Chinese cabbage, shredded
1 red pepper, deseeded and thinly sliced
1 large red chilli, deseeded and thinly sliced
125 g (4 oz) smoked tofu, diced
a handful each of fresh mint and coriander leaves

Dressing:
4 tbsp rice wine vinegar
2 tbsp water
1 tbsp caster sugar
2 star anise
2 tbsp light soy sauce
1 tsp sesame oil

Make the dressing: put the vinegar, water, sugar and star anise into a saucepan and heat gently to dissolve the sugar. Simmer for 4–5 minutes until reduced by half and remove from the heat. Leave to cool and then stir in the soy sauce and sesame oil.

Cut the carrot and cucumber into small batons and place in a large bowl with the cabbage, pepper, chilli, tofu and herbs. Add the dressing, stir well until evenly coated and serve at once.

CORIANDER YOGURT DIP WITH VEGETABLE CRUDITÉS

Serves: 4
Preparation time: 15 minutes

Use whatever vegetables you like to accompany this delicious spiced yogurt dip. The dip will keep well for 24 hours in the fridge – cover with clingfilm.

650 g (1$^1/_4$ lb) selection of mixed vegetables, such as baby carrots, red peppers, blanched asparagus, cherry tomatoes

Coriander yogurt dip:
1 bunch of fresh coriander leaves
1 large green chilli, deseeded and finely chopped
1 garlic clove, crushed
2 tbsp cold water
250 ml (8 fl oz) Greek-style yogurt
1 tbsp lemon juice
salt

Prepare the vegetables, peeling and deseeding them as necessary, and cut into large chunks. Arrange the vegetables on a large platter.

Make the dip: place the coriander, chilli, garlic and water in a food processor and process until as smooth as possible. Transfer to a bowl, stir in the yogurt and lemon juice and season to taste. Serve with the vegetables.

ROASTED SWEET POTATO AND RICOTTA FILO TART

Serves: 2
Preparation time: 15 minutes
Cooking time: 55-60 minutes

Make this tart ahead of time and reheat in a low oven for 20 minutes to serve warm.

500 g (1 lb) sweet potato, diced
1 red onion, cut into thin wedges
1 tbsp chopped fresh sage
2 tbsp olive oil
6 large sheets filo pastry
25 g (1 oz) butter, melted
250 g (8 oz) ricotta
150 ml ($^1/_4$ pint) single cream
2 eggs, lightly beaten
50 g (2 oz) freshly grated Parmesan cheese
salt and pepper
50 g (2 oz) pitted black olives

Preheat the oven to 220°C/425°F/Gas Mark 7. Put the sweet potato, onion, sage, olive oil and some salt and pepper into a small roasting tin, stir well and roast for 30 minutes or until the potato and onions are tender. Leave to cool.

Cut the pastry sheets crossways in half and lay flat. Brush with butter, top with a second sheet and brush this with butter. Repeat with the remaining sheets and then transfer the pastry to a 20 cm/8 in square deep flan tin or roasting tin, pressing gently into the base and sides of the tin.

Scatter the cooked vegetables into the pastry case. Beat the ricotta, cream, eggs, Parmesan and a little seasoning together and pour over the vegetables. Top with the olives and bake for 20-25 minutes until the pastry is golden and the fillings puffed up and firm to the touch. Leave to cool and serve warm.

CARAMELIZED ONION AND GOAT'S CHEESE TART

Serves: 4–6
Preparation time: 20 minutes, plus chilling
Cooking time: 40–45 minutes

Use a soft goat cheese without a rind, or, if you prefer, use feta instead.
The pastry can be made several hours ahead, or in advance and frozen.

40 g (1^1/$_2$ oz) butter
2 onions, finely sliced
1 garlic clove, crushed
2 tsp chopped fresh sage
salt and pepper
125 g (4 oz) soft goat's cheese, crumbled
200 g (7 oz) crème fraîche
2 eggs, lightly beaten

Pastry:
175 g (6 oz) plain flour
a pinch of salt
75 g (3 oz) butter, diced
3 tbsp cold water

Preheat the oven to 200°C/400°F/Gas Mark 6. Make the pastry by
sifting the flour and salt into a bowl and rubbing in the butter until the mixture
resembles fine breadcrumbs. Gradually work in the water to form a soft
dough. Knead gently and shape into a disc. Wrap in clingfilm and chill for
20 minutes.

Roll the dough out on a lightly floured surface and use to line a 23 cm/
9 in flan tin. Prick the base with a fork and chill for a further 20 minutes. Line
the case with baking paper and baking beans and bake for 15 minutes.
Remove the paper and beans and bake for a further 8–10 minutes until
the pastry is crisp and golden. Leave to cool.

Melt the butter in a frying pan and gently fry the onions, garlic, sage, salt
and pepper for 15–20 minutes until the onions are caramelized. Leave to cool.

Beat the goat's cheese, crème fraîche and eggs together until smooth
and season lightly. Spoon the cooked onions into the pastry case and pour
over the crème fraîche mixture. Bake for 20–25 minutes until puffed up and
golden. Leave to cool slightly and serve warm with a mixed salad.

CHICKPEAS, SPINACH AND TOMATOES

Serves: 4
Preparation time: 5 minutes
Cooking time: 15 minutes

This makes a lovely vegetarian supper dish served with rice or can be served as part of a spread.

2 tbsp extra virgin olive oil
1 onion, finely chopped
2 garlic cloves, crushed
2 tsp ground coriander
1 tsp ground cumin
$1/2$ tsp ground ginger
2 x 400 g (13 oz) cans chickpeas, drained
1 x 400 g (13 oz) can chopped tomatoes
300 ml ($1/2$ pint) vegetable stock
salt and pepper
250 g (8 oz) baby spinach leaves

To serve:
hot chilli sauce
natural yogurt
pitta bread

Heat the oil in a saucepan and gently fry the onion, garlic and spices for 5 minutes. Add the chickpeas, tomatoes, stock and salt and pepper to taste. Bring to the boil and simmer gently, uncovered, for 15 minutes.

Stir in the spinach leaves and cook gently until wilted. Serve the chickpeas with a little chilli sauce, yogurt and pitta bread.

BAKED AUBERGINE LASAGNE

Serves: 4
Preparation time: 10 minutes
Cooking time: 40–50 minutes

This is the perfect vegetarian alternative to a meat lasagne. The quick tomato sauce can also be served with freshly cooked pasta as a simple supper dish. The lasagne can be assembled several hours ahead of time, to be baked later. You may need to increase the cooking time by up to 15 minutes.

2 large aubergines (about 450 g/15 oz each)
3 tbsp extra virgin olive oil
250 g (8 oz) grated mozzarella cheese
25 g (1 oz) freshly grated Parmesan cheese

Quick tomato sauce:
2 x 400 g (13 oz) cans chopped tomatoes
3 garlic cloves, finely chopped
4 tbsp extra virgin olive oil
2 tbsp chopped fresh basil
1 tsp caster sugar
$1/4$ tsp dried red chilli flakes
salt and pepper

green salad and crusty bread, to serve

Make the tomato sauce: place all the ingredients in a saucepan and bring to the boil and simmer gently, uncovered, for 20–25 minutes until the sauce is thickened. Season to taste.

Preheat the oven to 200°C/400°F/Gas Mark 6 and grease a 20 x 30cm/8 x 12 in baking dish. Preheat the grill to high. Cut the aubergines into thin slices, brush the slices with oil and season with a little salt and pepper. Grill for 2–3 minutes each side until charred and softened.

Layer the aubergine slices, tomato sauce and mozzarella in the prepared baking dish to give three layers of each, finishing with the cheese. Scatter over the Parmesan and bake for 20–25 minutes until bubbling and golden. Serve with a crisp green salad and crusty bread.

BEETROOT AND FETA RISOTTO

Serves: 4
Preparation time: 15 minutes
Cooking time: 35–40 minutes

A good risotto should be creamy, with the rice retaining a slight crunch in the middle. Stirring the rice constantly as it cooks may sound laborious, but is in fact very satisfying and what gives a risotto its characteristic creamy texture.

> 1.2 litres (2 pints) vegetable stock
> 50 g (2 oz) butter
> 1 onion, finely chopped
> 2 garlic cloves, crushed
> 2 tsp chopped fresh thyme
> 350 g (12 oz) raw beetroots, finely chopped
> 350 g (12 oz) arborio rice
> 150 ml ($^1/_4$ pint) red wine
> 125 g (4 oz) feta cheese, crumbled
> 25 g (1 oz) freshly grated Parmesan cheese
> salt and pepper

Pour the stock into a saucepan and bring to a gentle simmer. Meanwhile, melt the butter in a saucepan and gently fry the onion, garlic and thyme for 5 minutes. Add the beetroot and a little salt and pepper and fry for a further 5 minutes until the onion is softened.

Add the rice, stir-fry for 30 seconds until the grains are glossy and then add the wine. Simmer until the wine is absorbed, then add a ladleful of the simmering stock. Cook gently, stirring for 5 minutes or until the stock is absorbed. Continue adding the stock and stirring for 20–25 minutes until the rice is tender and all the stock absorbed.

Stir in the feta and Parmesan and adjust seasonings. Cover and leave to rest for 5 minutes. Serve hot.

CHILLI BEAN AND VEGETABLE STEW

Serves: 4
Preparation time: 20 minutes
Cooking time: 45–50 minutes

Increase the amount of chilli powder according to taste. Passata is a strained tomato sauce available from most supermarkets. This chilli bean stew can be made up to a day ahead and reheated for serving.

> 4 tbsp olive oil
> 1 onion, chopped
> 2 garlic cloves, crushed
> 2 large potatoes, diced (about 250 g/8 oz each)
> 1 red pepper, deseeded and diced
> 2 tsp ground coriander
> 1 tsp ground cumin
> 1/2 tsp hot chilli powder
> 600 ml (1 pint) passata
> 2 x 400 g (13 oz) cans red kidney beans
> 450 ml (3/4 pint) water
> salt and pepper
> 250 g (8 oz) button mushrooms
> 2 tbsp chopped fresh coriander
>
> To serve:
> plain boiled rice
> diced avocado
> sour cream

Heat half the oil in a saucepan and fry the onion and garlic for 5 minutes. Add the potatoes, pepper and spices and fry for a further 5 minutes, until the onion is softened. Add the passata, kidney beans, water and salt and pepper to taste. Bring to the boil, cover and simmer gently for 20 minutes.

Heat the remaining oil in a frying pan and fry the mushrooms for 4–5 minutes until browned, add to the chilli with the coriander and cook for a further 10–15 minutes until the vegetables are tender. Serve with boiled rice, diced avocado and sour cream.

THAI-STYLE VEGETABLE CURRY

Serves: 4
Preparation time: 15 minutes
Cooking time: 20 minutes

1 tbsp sunflower oil
1 tbsp Thai red curry paste
600 ml (1 pint) vegetable stock
1 x 400 ml (14 fl oz) can coconut milk
2 tbsp fish sauce
1 tbsp soft brown sugar
6 Kaffir lime leaves, bruised
750 g (1 lb) mixed fresh vegetables, such as cauliflower,
    broccoli, sweetcorn and mangetout
200 g (7 oz) frozen peas
200 g (7 oz) firm tofu, diced
juice of 1 lime

To garnish:
shredded lime leaves
coriander leaves

boiled rice, to serve

Heat the oil in a saucepan and stir-fry the paste over a low heat for 30 seconds. Stir in the stock, coconut milk, fish sauce, sugar and lime leaves, bring to the boil and simmer gently for 5 minutes.

Chop the larger vegetables. Add to the pan, then stir in the peas, tofu and lime juice and simmer for a further 4–5 minutes until the vegetables are cooked. Spoon into bowls and top with shredded lime leaves and coriander leaves. Serve with plain boiled rice.

ASIAN VEGETABLE STIR-FRY

Serves: 4
Preparation time: 25 minutes
Cooking time: 6–7 minutes

When stir-frying vegetables, it is important not to overcook them, they should always retain a good crunch.

350 g (12 oz) cauliflower, cut into florets
200 g (7 oz) green beans, halved
3 tbsp sunflower oil
2 tsp freshly grated root ginger
2 garlic cloves, sliced
1/4 tsp dried red chilli flakes
1 large carrot, sliced
1 large courgette, sliced
125 g (4 oz) baby sweetcorn, halved lengthways
1 red onion, sliced

Sauce:
150 ml (1/4 pint) vegetable stock
4 tbsp light soy sauce
2 tsp sesame oil
2 tsp cornflour
2 tsp caster sugar

To garnish:
coriander leaves
sliced red chilli

Make the sauce by combining the ingredients in a bowl and set aside.

Blanch the cauliflower and green beans in a large saucepan of lightly salted, boiling water for 2 minutes. Drain and refresh under cold water, drain again and dry on kitchen paper.

Heat the oil in a wok or large frying pan and, as soon as it begins smoking, reduce the heat to medium. Add the ginger, garlic and chilli flakes and stir-fry for 10 seconds, then add the cauliflower, beans and carrots and stir-fry for 1 minute.

Add the courgette, sweetcorn and onion and stir-fry for 1 minute. Pour in the sauce and cook for a further 1 minute until the vegetables are just tender. Transfer to a large platter and serve garnished with coriander leaves and red chilli.

BULGHAR WHEAT PATTIES WITH TAHINI SAUCE

Serves: 4
Preparation time: 30 minutes, plus soaking
Cooking time: 20 minutes

75 g (3 oz) bulghar wheat
250 g (8 oz) potatoes, cubed
1 tbsp olive oil
1 small onion, finely chopped
1 garlic clove, crushed
1 tsp ground cumin
75 g (3 oz) grated Cheddar cheese
25 g (1 oz) hazelnuts, finely chopped
2 tbsp chopped fresh coriander
1 egg, lightly beaten
4 tbsp plain flour
salt and pepper

Tahini sauce:
125 g (4 oz) Greek-style yogurt
1 tbsp tahini paste
1 garlic clove, crushed
1 tbsp lemon juice
salt and pepper

vegetable oil, for shallow frying
rocket salad, to serve

Put the bulghar wheat in a bowl, add boiling water to cover by 2.5 cm/1 in and set aside to soak for 20 minutes until the bulghar wheat is tender. Drain well.

Boil the potatoes for 10–15 minutes until tender, drain well and mash with a potato masher. Heat the oil in a frying pan and fry the onion, garlic and cumin for 10 minutes until the onion is softened.

Mix together the bulghar wheat, mashed potato, onion mixture, cheese, hazelnuts, coriander, egg, flour and salt and pepper. Work together until evenly combined and, using wet hands, shape into 8 patties.

Make the sauce: combine the ingredients in a bowl and season to taste.

Fry the patties in oil for 5 minutes each side and serve with the sauce and a rocket salad.

MIXED MUSHROOM AND PASTA BAKE

Porcini is the Italian name for a variety of mushroom which is often sold dried. Although expensive, dried porcini are used in minute quantities because of their intense flavour (they keep for ages). Make sure you cut the fresh mushrooms into even sized pieces so they cook evenly. This dish can be assembled ahead of time, to be cooked later.

5 g ($^{1}/_{4}$ oz) dried porcini
3 tbsp boiling water
350 g (12 oz) dried penne
4 tbsp extra virgin olive oil
1 onion, finely chopped
2 garlic cloves, crushed
2 tsp chopped fresh sage
500 g (1 lb) mixed mushrooms, sliced
450 ml ($^{3}/_{4}$ pint) single cream
250 g (8 oz) mozzarella, diced
50 g (2 oz) freshly grated Parmesan cheese
salt and pepper

garlic bread, to serve

Preheat the oven to 200°C/400°F/Gas Mark 6 and grease a 20x30 cm/8x12 in baking dish. Soak the porcini in boiling water for 15 minutes, then drain and chop the porcini. Reserve the soaking liquid.

Cook the pasta according to the packet instructions until al dente (just cooked). Drain well and place in a large bowl.

Heat the oil in a frying pan and gently fry the onion, garlic and sage for 5 minutes. Add the mushrooms and soaked porcini, increase the heat and fry for a further 5 minutes until the mushrooms are golden. Add to the pasta with the cream, reserved porcini liquid, mozzarella, Parmesan and salt and pepper and stir well. Transfer to the prepared baking dish and bake for 20–25 minutes until bubbling and golden. Serve with garlic bread.

PASTA WITH BROCCOLI AND GARLIC BREADCRUMBS

Serves: 4
Preparation time: 20 minutes
Cooking time: 20 minutes

500 g (1 lb) broccoli
500 g (1 lb) dried orrechiette or other pasta shapes
6 tbsp extra virgin olive oil
grated zest and juice of 1 unwaxed lemon
$\frac{1}{4}$ tsp dried chilli flakes
25 g (1 oz) toasted pine nuts
50 g (2 oz) sultanas
2 tbsp capers, drained and rinsed
2 tbsp chopped fresh basil
salt and pepper

Garlic breadcrumbs:
4 tbsp extra virgin olive oil
125 g (4 oz) fresh white breadcrumbs
2 garlic cloves, crushed

grated Parmesan cheese, to serve

Make the garlic breadcrumbs: heat the oil in a frying pan and stir-fry the breadcrumbs for 4 minutes. Add the garlic and cook for a further 1–2 minutes until the breadcrumbs are crisp and golden. Transfer to a bowl and set aside. Wipe the pan clean.

Blanch the broccoli in a pan of lightly salted, boiling water for 3 minutes, drain well, refresh under cold water and dry thoroughly on kitchen paper. Cook the pasta according to packet instructions. Drain, reserving 2 tablespoons of cooking liquid and return to the pan.

Heat the oil in a frying pan, add the garlic, lemon zest and chilli and fry gently for 1 minute until softened, but not browned. Add the broccoli and cook for 2 minutes, then add the pine nuts, sultanas, capers, basil and lemon juice and cook for 1 minute. Stir the broccoli mixture into the pasta with the reserved cooking water and stir over a medium heat for a further 1 minute until heated through.

Serve the pasta topped with the garlic breadcrumbs and Parmesan.

FRUIT

The main ingredients that you will need to make any of the following recipes are highlighted in the fridge. Extra ingredients to serve or flavour are shown on the list below.

BLUEBERRIES
PEACHES
APRICOTS
CHERRIES
PLUMS
PUDDING RICE
COCONUT MILK
ALMOND ESSENCE
VANILLA POD
BANANAS
CLEAR HONEY
APRICOT JAM
BLUEBERRY JAM
SHREDDED COCONUT
GROUND ALMONDS
GROUND CINNAMON
FRUITY RED WINE
SAUTERNES
LIMONCELLO
BRIOCHE
BELGIAN WAFFLES
PISTACHIO NUTS
ROSEWATER
PUFF PASTRY
WHITE WINE VINEGAR
CORNFLOUR

HONEYED BANANAS WITH
COCONUT RISOTTO

Serves: 4
Preparation time: 5 minutes
Cooking time: 25 minutes

A sweet risotto similar to rice pudding, with a hint of coconut, which is both delicious and comforting.

175 g (6 oz) pudding rice
500 ml (15 fl oz) milk
400 ml (14 fl oz) coconut milk
75 g (3 oz) caster sugar
50 g (2 oz) unsalted butter
3 large bananas, thickly sliced
2 tbsp clear honey

shredded coconut, toasted

Put the rice into a saucepan and cover with plenty of cold water. Bring to the boil and cook for 5 minutes, drain the rice and return to the pan. Add the milk, coconut milk and sugar and bring to the boil. Reduce the heat and simmer gently, stirring frequently, for 20–25 minutes until the rice is cooked and the liquid absorbed. Spoon into warmed bowls.

Melt the butter in a frying pan and fry the banana slices for 30 seconds each side. Add the honey, toss until evenly coated and spoon the bananas over the rice. Top with a little toasted coconut and serve at once.

FIG AND ALMOND TART

Serves: 4–6
Preparation time: 15 minutes, plus chilling
Cooking time: 52 minutes

150 g (5 oz) plain flour
a pinch of salt
75g (3 oz) unsalted butter, diced
2 tbsp caster sugar
2 egg yolks
1 tbsp cold water

Filling:
75 g (3 oz) unsalted butter, softened
75 g (3 oz) ground almonds
75g (3 oz) caster sugar
2 tbsp double cream
2 tsp ground cinnamon
2 tsp lemon juice
a few drops of almond essence
500 g (1 lb) fresh figs, quartered

crème fraîche, to serve

Sift the flour and salt into a bowl and rub in the butter until the mixture resembles fine breadcrumbs. Stir in the sugar and then work in the egg yolks and water to form a soft dough. Shape into a disc and wrap in cling film. Chill for 20 minutes. Roll out the dough on a lightly floured surface and use to line a 23 cm/9 in fluted flan tin. Prick the base and chill for a further 20 minutes.

Preheat the oven to 200°C/400°F/Gas Mark 6. Line the pastry with baking paper and baking beans and bake for 12 minutes. Remove the paper and beans and bake for a further 10 minutes until the pastry is golden. Leave to cool.

Make the filling: beat the butter, almonds, sugar, cream, cinnamon, lemon juice and almond essence together until smooth and spread half over the pastry. Arrange the figs on top and dot over the remaining almond cream, allowing the figs to poke through in places. Bake for 30 minutes until the topping is golden and firm. Remove from the oven, leave to cool slightly and serve warm with crème fraîche.

FREE-FORM PEACH AND BLUEBERRY TART

Serves: 6
Preparation time: 10 minutes, plus chilling
Cooking time: 30–35 minutes

Make the pastry in advance, wrap in clingfilm and chill for up to 4 hours. Return to room temperature for 30 minutes, roll out and use as required.

4 tbsp blueberry jam
4 peaches, quartered, stoned and thickly sliced
150 g (5 oz) blueberries
1 tbsp caster sugar
1 tsp ground cinnamon

Pastry:
200 g (7 oz) plain flour
^{1}/2 tsp salt
100 g (3^1/2 oz) chilled butter, diced
2 tbsp caster sugar
2 egg yolks
1–2 tbsp cold water

crème fraîche, to serve

Make the pastry: sift the flour into a bowl, add the salt and then rub in the butter until the mixture resembles breadcrumbs. Stir in the sugar and then gradually work in the egg yolks and enough water to form a soft dough. Shape into a disc, wrap in clingfilm and chill for 20 minutes.

Preheat the oven to 190°C/375°F/Gas Mark 5 and line a baking tray with baking paper. Roll out the pastry thinly to a 30cm/12 in round and transfer to the baking tray.

Spread the jam over the pastry, leaving a 5 cm/2 in border and arrange the peaches and blueberries over the top. Combine the sugar and cinnamon and scatter over the fruit.

Lift the pastry edges up and over the fruit to form a rim, pressing down firmly, but gently. Bake for 30–35 minutes until the pastry is golden and the fruit softened. Serve warm with crème fraîche.

SUMMER BERRY BRIOCHE

Serves: 4
Preparation time: 5 minutes
Cooking time: 10 minutes, plus cooling

Brioche loaf is available from the bread section of most larger
supermarkets; alternatively you could use panettone or raisin bread. The
fruits can be prepared ahead of time and chilled until required.

> 300 ml ($1/2$ pint) fruity red wine
> 75 g (3 oz) caster sugar
> 50 ml (2 fl oz) orange juice
> 1 vanilla pod, split
> 2 strips of lemon zest
> 500 g (1 lb) mixed summer berries, such as raspberries,
>   blueberries and strawberries
> 4 slices of brioche
>
> whipped cream, to serve

Place the red wine, sugar, orange juice, vanilla pod and lemon zest in a
saucepan and bring to the boil. Simmer for 6–8 minutes until reduced by
half and the sauce is thick and syrupy. Place the berries in a bowl, pour
over the hot syrup and leave to cool for 30 minutes.

Toast the brioche slices and place on serving plates. Top with the
berries and syrup and serve with a dollop of whipped cream.

CHILLED MELON AND RASPBERRIES WITH SAUTERNES

Serves: 4
Preparation time: 5 minutes
Chilling time: 30 minutes

A simple and refreshing dessert. Sauternes is a French dessert wine with an intense fruit flavour that complements the melon and raspberries perfectly.

2 Cantaloupe or Charantais melons, halved
150 g (5 oz) raspberries
200 ml (7 fl oz) Sauternes

Scoop out and discard the melon seeds and place the halves on plates. Scatter raspberries into the hollows and pour in the Sauternes. Chill for 30 minutes before serving.

FRUIT SALAD WITH ROSEWATER SYRUP

Serves: 4
Preparation time: 15 minutes, plus marinating
Cooking time: 5 minutes, plus cooling

Rosewater is a North African flavouring added to both sweet and savoury dishes. It adds a wonderfully fragrant flavour to this fruit salad which looks very pretty decorated with a few pink rose petals.

2 oranges, peeled and cut into thin slices
6 apricots, halved and stoned
250 g (8 oz) strawberries, hulled and halved
250 g (8 oz) cherries
1 tbsp pistachio nuts, finely chopped

Rosewater syrup:
200 ml (7 fl oz) water
100 g (3^1/$_2$ oz) caster sugar
1 tbsp orange juice
1 tbsp lemon juice
2 tsp rosewater

rose petals, to decorate (optional)

Make the syrup: heat the water, sugar and orange juice together in a small saucepan until the sugar dissolves. Increase the heat and simmer gently for 5 minutes until the syrup is thickened. Remove from the heat, add the lemon juice and rosewater and set aside until cold.

Place the fruits in a shallow dish, pour over the syrup and marinate for 15 minutes. Scatter over the pistachio nuts and rose petals, if using, and serve at once.

POACHED PEARS WITH WAFFLES AND CHOCOLATE SAUCE

Serves: 4
Preparation time: 15 minutes, plus cooling
Cooking time: 20 minutes

Waffles are available fresh from the bread section of most larger supermarkets. Poach the pears up to 24 hours in advance and store in their syrup until required. Heat gently, still in their syrup, for 10–15 minutes until the pears are warm.

300 ml (1 pint) water
150 g (5 oz) caster sugar
pared zest and juice of 1 unwaxed lemon
4 firm, ripe pears, quartered and cored
100 g (3$1/2$ oz) plain chocolate, chopped
50 g (2 oz) unsalted butter, diced
2 tbsp single cream
8 Belgian waffles

Preheat the oven to 180°C/350°F/Gas Mark 4. Put the water, sugar, lemon zest and juice in a saucepan and heat gently to dissolve the sugar. Add the pear quarters, bring to the boil and simmer gently, partially covered, for 15 minutes until the pears are tender. Remove the pears from their syrup and leave to cool for 15 minutes.

Combine the chocolate, butter and cream in a bowl set over a saucepan of gently simmering water. Stir frequently until the chocolate has melted and the mixture is smooth.

Heat the waffles in the oven for 5 minutes and arrange on plates. Top with the pears, pour over the chocolate sauce and serve at once.

LITTLE PLUM PUDDINGS

Serves: 4
Preparation time: 5 minutes
Cooking time: 30 minutes

These little cakes also taste good served cold, so make ahead of time if
you wish.

>4 ripe plums, halved and stoned
>65 g (2^1/$_2$ oz) butter, softened (plus extra for greasing)
>65 g (2^1/$_2$ oz) soft brown sugar
>2 eggs, lightly beaten
>125 g (4 oz) self-raising flour, sifted
>^{1}/$_2$ tsp ground cinnamon
>2 tbsp soured cream
>
>extra soured cream, to serve

Preheat the oven to 180°C/350°F/Gas Mark 4 and butter
4 x 250 ml/8 fl oz timbales or ramekins. Place 2 plum halves skin-side
down in each dish.

Beat the butter and sugar together until light and fluffy. Gradually
beat in the eggs a little at a time until blended, then fold in the flour,
cinnamon and soured cream to form a dropping consistency. Spoon into
the moulds, covering the plums, and smooth the surface.

Place the dishes in a roasting tin and pour in enough boiling water
to reach half way up their sides. Bake for 30 minutes, remove from the
oven and lift the puddings out of the water, being careful not to burn
yourself. Leave to cool in the containers for 10 minutes, run a small
palette knife around the inside of each one and unmould on to a plate.
Allow to cool and serve warm with a dollop of soured cream.

FRENCH-STYLE APPLE FLAN

Serves: 6
Preparation time: 20 minutes
Cooking time: 30–35 minutes

This flan can be made ahead of time and warmed through (at 190°C/375°F/Gas Mark 5) for 15 minutes or until warm.

1 x 350 g (12 oz) block puff pastry, thawed if frozen
100 g (3^1/$_2$ oz) apricot jam
2 tsp water
2 dessert apples, Granny Smith's or Golden Delicious
2 tsp caster sugar
15 g (^{1}/$_2$ oz) unsalted butter, chilled

crème fraîche, to serve

Preheat the oven to 220°C/425°F/Gas Mark 7 and place an oven tray on the middle shelf to heat up. Roll out the pastry on a lightly floured surface to a 20x30 cm/8x12 in rectangle and, using a sharp knife, score a 1 cm/^{1}/$_2$ in border around the edges. Prick the pastry with a fork, place on a baking tray and flute the edges.

Put the jam and water into a small saucepan and heat gently, stirring until melted. Brush a quarter over the surface of the pastry.

Slice the apples thinly and arrange over the jam in overlapping rows. Brush with the remaining jam and scatter over the sugar. Grate over the butter and bake on the hot oven tray for 30–35 minutes until the pastry and apples are golden. Serve warm, with crème fraîche.

MANGO AND PASSIONFRUIT PAVLOVA

Serves: 6–8
Preparation time: 10 minutes
Cooking time: 1–1¹/₂ hours

When making meringues, make sure you beat well after each addition of sugar so that the mixture is really stiff. Meringues keep well if stored in an airtight container for up to 3 days.

> 3 egg whites
> 175 g (6 oz) caster sugar
> 1 tsp white wine vinegar
> 1 tsp cornflour
> 300 ml (¹/₂ pint) double cream
> 2 ripe mangoes, peeled, stoned and sliced
> 4 ripe passionfruit, halved
>
> icing sugar, to dust

Preheat the oven to 130°C/250°F/Gas Mark 1/2 and line a large baking tray with baking paper. Draw around a 23 cm/9 in plate to form a template.

Put the egg whites in a clean, dry bowl and, using an electric beater, whisk the egg whites until stiff. Gradually whisk in the sugar 1 tablespoon at a time, whisking well after each addition until the mixture is thick and glossy. Fold in the vinegar and cornflour.

Spoon the meringue mixture on to the baking paper, spreading it to the edges of the circle, and form a dip in the centre. Bake in the middle of the oven for 1–1¹/₂ hours until set but still slightly soft in the centre. Remove from the oven and leave to cool in a draught-free place.

Peel the paper away carefully from the base of the pavlova and place on a large plate. Whip the cream until stiff and spoon into the hollow centre. Top with the mango slices and passionfruit pulp and serve dusted with icing sugar.

ICED LEMON AND LIMONCELLO SHERBET

Serves: 4
Preparation time: 5 minutes
Cooking time: 10 minutes, plus chilling
Freezing time: 2–2^1/$_2$ hours

Limoncello is an Italian lemon-flavoured liqueur and is available from good
liquor shops. Lemon-flavoured vodka could be used instead. The mixture is
frozen until it is really icy like a slush puppy. This will keep frozen for up to
1 month. Remove from the freezer for 20 minutes, before serving.

> 175 g (6 oz) caster sugar
> 300 ml (^{1}/$_2$ pint) water
> 200 ml (7 fl oz) lemon juice (from about 6 lemons)
> 2 tbsp limoncello, plus extra to serve

Place the sugar and water in a saucepan, heat gently to dissolve the
sugar, then bring to the boil. Simmer for 5 minutes, remove from the heat
and leave to cool.

Stir the lemon juice and limoncello into the sugar syrup and transfer to
a bowl. Place in the freezer and then whisk every 15 minutes or so for
about 2 hours, and then about every 30 minutes until the mixture is slushy
and almost frozen.

Spoon into iced glasses, pour a little limoncello over each one and
serve at once.

EGGS AND DAIRY

Your weekly shop will include eggs and dairy products from which, with the help of your store cupboard, you can make any of the dishes below. The main fresh ingredients are highlighted in the fridge. Any extra flavourings, seasonings and side dishes are listed below.

ONION
GARLIC
FRESH MIXED HERBS
FRESH RASPBERRIES
CLEAR MAPLE SYRUP
WALNUTS
DRIED FIGS
HAZELNUTS
PISTACHIO NUTS
FLAKED ALMONDS
VANILLA ESSENCE
WHOLE NUTMEG
NUTELLA
CHOCOLATE SPONGE
MADE CUSTARD
VANILLA POD
CORNFLOUR
GELATINE
BLUEBERRIES
LIGHT BEER
FRANGELICO OR AMARETTO LIQUEUR
KIRSCH
MARSALA OR SWEET SHERRY
BAGUETTE
DESSERT BISCUITS
VANILLA ICE CREAM

CHEESE AND BEER FONDUE WITH GARLIC BREAD

Serves: 4
Preparation time: 5 minutes
Cooking time: 15 minutes

A blast from the past! A cheese fondue is such fun because we all get to do our own cooking. If you don't have a fondue set, you can use the saucepan in which the sauce was made – remember to put two thick mats on the table as the base of the pan will be hot.

> 1 large baguette, sliced
> 2 garlic cloves, crushed
> 125 g (4 oz) butter, softened
> 150 ml (¼ pint) light beer
> 500 g (1 lb) Gruyère cheese, grated
> 2 tsp cornflour
> 2 tbsp Kirsch (cherry liqueur)

Preheat the oven to 200°C/400°F/Gas Mark 6. Arrange the bread slices on 2 baking trays. Beat the garlic and butter together, spread a little over each slice of bread and bake for 6–8 minutes until crisp and golden. Remove from the oven.

Pour the beer into a saucepan and heat gently until warm. Add the cheese and stir over a low heat for 5 minutes until the cheese is melted. Combine the cornflour and Kirsch in a small bowl, and stir into the melted cheese mixture. Increase the heat and allow the mixture to just reach boiling point, then immediately remove from the heat.

Transfer the cheese to the fondue pan, set on the heated burners, and place in the centre of the table. Thread the garlic bread slices onto fondue skewers and dunk into the melted cheese.

BACON, TOMATO AND FETA TART

Serves: 4
Preparation time: 20 minutes, plus chilling
Cooking time: 50 minutes

This is a modern version of a quiche Lorraine. Feta is a strongly flavoured cheese, but, if you prefer, you can use a milder cheese such as ricotta or cream cheese. This tart can be made several hours in advance and served cold, or you can bake the pastry case ahead of time until ready to fill.

150 g (5 oz) plain flour
a pinch of salt
50 g (2 oz) butter, diced
15 g ($\frac{1}{2}$ oz) freshly grated Parmesan cheese
1 egg yolk
2 tbsp cold water

For the filling:
1 tbsp olive oil
125 g (4 oz) smoked bacon, diced
1 tsp chopped fresh thyme
125 g (4 oz) cherry tomatoes, halved
125 g (4 oz) feta cheese, diced
3 eggs, lightly beaten
200 ml ($\frac{1}{2}$ pint) double cream
salt and pepper

Sift the flour and salt in to a bowl and rub in the butter until the mixture resembles fine breadcrumbs. Add the Parmesan and work in the egg yolk and water to form a soft dough. Knead lightly, wrap and chill for 20 minutes. Roll out the dough on a lightly floured surface and use to line a 23 cm/9 in flan tin. Chill for a further 20 minutes.

Preheat the oven to 200°C/400°F/Gas Mark 6. Line the pastry case with baking paper and baking beans and bake for 15 minutes. Remove the baking paper and beans and bake for a further 10 minutes until the pastry is crisp. Set aside to cool.

Prepare the filling. Heat the oil in a frying pan and fry the bacon and thyme for 5 minutes until lightly golden. Scatter over the base of the pastry case and add the tomatoes. Beat the remaining ingredients together and pour into the case. Bake for 20 minutes until golden and set. Cool slightly and serve warm.

CARAMELISED CAMEMBERT WITH WALNUTS

Serves: 4
Preparation time: 5 minutes
Cooking time: 7–8 minutes

This is like an instant fondue – the creamy centre melts and oozes as it cooks, breaking through the rind to make a perfect gooey melted sauce that is ideal for dunking.

1 x 200 g (7 oz) Camembert
1–2 tbsp clear maple syrup
a few chopped walnuts

To serve:
sliced French bread
apple wedges

Preheat the grill to high. Line a baking tray with foil and place the Camembert on top. Grill (about 5 cm/2 in away from the heat source) for 6–7 minutes or until soft and the rind is beginning to puff and brown.

Remove from the grill, drizzle with maple syrup and scatter with the walnuts and cook for a further 1 minute until the syrup bubbles and begins to caramelise.

Transfer to a platter and serve with sliced French bread or apple wedges to dip.

YORKSHIRE PUDDINGS

Makes: 8
Preparation time: 5 minutes, plus resting
Cooking time: 25–30 minutes

Although they are the perfect accompaniment to roast beef, you can serve Yorkshire puds with any roast meat. The batter can go into the oven once the meat is cooked and resting. Remember, never open the door while the batter is rising or it will collapse, never to rise again.

125 g (4 oz) plain flour
$1/2$ tsp salt
300 ml ($1/2$ pint) milk
2 eggs, lightly beaten
1 tbsp chopped fresh rosemary or thyme
sunflower oil

Preheat the oven to 220°C/425°F/Gas Mark 7. Sift the flour and salt into a bowl and make a well in the middle. Gradually whisk in the milk and eggs to form a smooth batter with a consistency similar to pouring cream. Add the rosemary or thyme and set aside for 30 minutes.

Pour about $1/2$ tablespoon of oil into 8 holes of a muffin tray and place in the oven for 5 minutes until the oil is really hot. Carefully ladle or pour in the prepared batter and bake for 20–25 minutes until the batter is puffed up and golden. Serve hot.

BAKED MUSHROOM AND THYME FRITTATA

Serves: 4
Preparation time: 10 minutes
Cooking time: 28 minutes

This can be made several hours ahead of time, to be served cold. Chill until required and return to room temperature for 1 hour before serving.

>   2 tbsp extra virgin olive oil
>   1 onion, finely chopped
>   2 garlic cloves, crushed
>   1 tbsp chopped fresh thyme
>   350 g (12 oz) mushrooms, sliced
>   6 eggs
>   2 tbsp milk
>   salt and pepper
>   2 tbsp freshly grated Parmesan cheese

Preheat the oven to 200°C/400°F/Gas Mark 6 and grease a 20cm/8 in square baking dish. Heat the oil in a frying pan and gently fry the onion, garlic and thyme for 5 minutes until softened. Add the mushrooms and stir-fry for 2–3 minutes until browned and just starting to soften.

Beat the eggs with the milk, salt and pepper. Stir in the mushroom mixture and pour into the prepared baking dish. Scatter over the Parmesan and bake for 20 minutes until firm in the centre. Leave to cool. Serve warm or cold, cut into slices

LEMON CREAMS WITH CRUSHED PISTACHIO TOFFEE

Serves: 4
Preparation time: 5 minutes
Cooking time: 8 minutes, plus chilling overnight

When making the toffee it is important not to burn the caramel. The sugar will melt and bubble and after a few minutes begin to darken; remove it from the heat as soon as it becomes a deep golden brown. The creams can be made up to 24 hours in advance. Chill until required.

> 100 g (3^1/$_2$ oz) granulated sugar
> 50 g (2 oz) shelled pistachio nuts
> 400 ml (14 fl oz) cream
> 100 g (3^1/$_2$ oz) caster sugar
> 100 ml (3^1/$_2$ fl oz) lemon juice

Line a baking tray with baking paper. Place the granulated sugar and nuts in a heavy-based saucepan and heat very gently, without stirring or moving the pan, until the sugar dissolves. Bring to the boil and cook for 3–5 minutes until the mixture turns a golden brown. Pour on to the prepared baking tray and leave to set.

Heat the cream and caster sugar together until the sugar dissolves, bring to the boil and simmer for 3 minutes. Remove the pan from the heat, add the lemon juice and immediately pour into four 200 ml/7 fl oz ramekins. Cool completely and then chill over night.

Break the pistachio toffee into pieces, place in a food processor and process until coarsely chopped. Scatter a little over each cream and serve.

RICH CHOCOLATE AND ROSEMARY MOUSSE

Serves: 4
Preparation time: 5 minutes, plus infusing
Cooking time: 3 minutes

These little pots of rosemary-flavoured chocolate mousse are rich, dark and totally wicked. They only require chilling for 30 minutes or so before they are firm enough to serve. If making them in advance, return to room temperature for about 30 minutes.

300 ml ($^1/_2$ pint) double cream
2 large rosemary sprigs, bashed
200 g (7 oz) dark chocolate
25 g (1 oz) caster sugar
2 eggs, separated

To decorate:
rosemary sprigs
icing sugar

dessert biscuits, to serve

Place the cream and rosemary sprigs in a saucepan and heat gently until boiling (make sure the cream doesn't boil over). Cook for 3 minutes, remove from the heat and leave to infuse for 20 minutes. Discard the rosemary sprigs and add the chocolate and sugar to the pan. Heat gently, stirring, until the chocolate is dissolved.

Remove the pan from the heat and leave to cool for 5 minutes. Transfer to a bowl and beat in the egg yolks. Whisk the egg whites in a separate bowl until stiff and fold into the chocolate mixture until evenly combined. Spoon the mousse into four 150 ml/$^1/_4$ pint cups or glasses and chill for 30 minutes or until firm.

Decorate the mousses with a rosemary sprig, dust with icing sugar and serve with dessert biscuits.

SPICED CUSTARD TART

Serves: 6
Preparation time: 10 minutes, plus chilling
Cooking time: 1 hour 25 minutes

Resting pastry after kneading and rolling allows it to relax after being stretched; this helps prevent it from shrinking as it bakes. Make and bake the pastry case up to 24 hours ahead of time. Prepare and bake the tart several hours in advance and serve warm or cold.

200 g (7 oz) plain flour
pinch of salt
125 g (4 oz) unsalted butter
25 g (1 oz) caster sugar
2 egg yolks
1–2 tbsp cold water

For the filling:
300 ml ($\frac{1}{2}$ pint) double cream
300 ml ($\frac{1}{2}$ pint) milk
3 eggs, plus 1 extra egg yolk
75 g (3 oz) soft brown sugar
1 tsp vanilla essence
1 whole nutmeg

raspberries, to serve (optional)

Sift the flour and salt into a bowl and rub in the butter until the mixture resembles breadcrumbs. Stir in the sugar and gradually work in the egg yolks and sufficient water to form a soft dough. Wrap and chill for 20 minutes. Roll out the dough on a lightly floured surface and use to line a 23 cm/9 in x 2.5 cm/1 in deep flan tin. Chill for a further 20 minutes.

Preheat the oven to 220°C/425°F/Gas Mark 7. Line the pastry case with baking paper and baking beans and bake for 15 minutes. Remove the baking paper and beans and bake blind for a further 10–12 minutes until the pastry is golden. Leave to cool. Reduce the oven to 150°C/300°F/Gas Mark 2.

Make the filling: beat together the cream, milk, eggs, egg yolk, sugar and vanilla essence and pour into the pastry case. Grate over a little nutmeg and bake for 50 minutes until just set. Remove from the oven and cool to room temperature. Serve warm or cold, with fresh raspberries, if wished.

NUTELLA AND FIG ICE CREAM PARFAITS

Serves: 4
Preparation time: 5 minutes
Freezing time: 2 hours

Frangelico is a hazelnut-flavoured liqueur available from all good liquor stores. Amaretto, which is almond-flavoured, can be used instead. The parfaits will keep frozen for up to 2 weeks.

500 g (1 lb) vanilla ice cream
125 g (4 oz) nutella
2 tbsp frangelico or ameretto liqueur
100 g (3$^{1}/_{2}$ oz) dried figs, roughly chopped
50 g (2 oz) hazelnuts, toasted

whipped cream, to serve

Remove the vanilla ice cream from the freezer and leave to return to room temperature and melt to a soft consistency. Place in a bowl and beat in the nutella and liqueur until smooth. Stir in the figs and hazelnuts and divide between four 200 ml/7 fl oz ramekins.

Freeze for 2 hours or until firm. To serve, dip the moulds briefly into hot water and turn out on to plates. Serve with a little whipped cream.

CHOCOLATE, MARSALA AND RASPBERRY TRIFLES

Serves: 4
Preparation time: 10 minutes, plus soaking
Chilling time: 30 minutes

Ready-made custard is available from the chilled cabinet of your local supermarket – look out for the rich creamier varieties. These trifles can be made and assembled several hours in advance.

125 g (4 oz) ready-made chocolate sponge
100 ml (3^1/$_2$ fl oz) Marsala or sweet sherry
250 g (8 oz) fresh raspberries
75 g (3 oz) white chocolate
200 m (7 fl oz) made custard
200 ml (7 fl oz) double cream
2 tbsp flaked almonds, toasted
2 tbsp grated dark chocolate (about 15g/^{1}/$_2$ oz)

Break the sponge cake into bite-sized pieces and divide between four large glasses. Sprinkle over the Marsala and leave to soak for 5 minutes. Spoon over 175 g/6 oz of the raspberries, reserving the rest for garnish.

Place the white chocolate in a bowl set over a saucepan of gently simmering water (do not allow the bottom of the bowl to touch the surface of the water, or the chocolate will burn) and heat gently until melted, stirring until smooth. Set aside to cool.

Pour the custard into a bowl and stir in the melted chocolate. Whip the cream in a separate bowl until stiff and fold into the custard mixture until combined. Spoon over the raspberries and chill for 30 minutes.

Decorate the trifles with the remaining raspberries, flaked almonds and grated dark chocolate. Serve at once.

VANILLA PANNA COTTA WITH BLUEBERRY SAUCE

Serves: 4
Preparation time: 5 minutes, plus chilling
Chilling time: 4 hours

Frozen blueberries can be used when fresh are unavailable. They can be cooked from frozen. The panna cotta and sauce can both be made up to 24 hours in advance. Serve the panna cotta straight from the fridge but return the sauce to room temperature 1 hour before serving.

> 600 ml (1 pint) double cream
> 1 vanilla pod, split
> 50 g (2 oz) caster sugar
> 2 tbsp water
> 1 1/2 tsp gelatine
>
> Blueberry sauce:
> 250 g (8 oz) blueberries
> 50 g (2 oz) caster sugar
> 2 tbsp water
> squeeze of lemon juice

Heat 450 ml/3/4 pint of the cream in a saucepan with the vanilla pod and sugar until the mixture just reaches boiling point. Remove from the heat, leave to cool and remove the vanilla pod, scraping the seeds into the milk.

Put the water into a small saucepan, sprinkle over the gelatine and leave to soak for 1 minute, then heat very gently until the gelatine dissolves. Do not allow the mixture to boil.

Whisk the remaining cream in a bowl until stiff, then whisk in the vanilla cream until evenly combined. Stir 2 tablespoons into the gelatine mixture and then stir that back into the bulk of the cream. Pour the mixture into four 200 ml/7 fl oz capacity ramekin dishes and chill until set.

Place the blueberries, sugar, water and lemon juice in a saucepan and heat gently to dissolve the sugar. Increase the heat and cook for 4–5 minutes until the blueberries are softened and the sauce becomes syrupy. Leave to cool.

Unmould the panna cotta by briefly immersing the ramekins in boiling water. Invert on to plates and serve with the sauce.

COOL EATING

RAID THE FRIDGE FOR RECIPES— EVERY DAY

Louise Pickford

Now that you have fallen in love with your fridge for sharing food with friends and family, you might like to try Cool Eating, Louise Pickford's cool inspiration for easy everyday meals.